Guide to PowerPoint

Mary Munter
Tuck School of Business
Dartmouth College

Dave Paradi
ThinkOutsideTheSlide.com

Upper Saddle River, New Jersey 07458

Library of Congress Cataloging-in-Publication Data

Munter, Mary
Guide to PowerPoint / by Mary Munter, Dave Paradi.—1st ed.
p. cm.
ISBN 0-13-145240-1
1. Presentation graphics software. 2. Microsoft PowerPoint (Computer file)
I. Paradi, Dave. II. Title.

T385.M864 2006
005.5'8—dc22 2006012143

Senior Acquisitions Editor: David Parker
VP/ Editorial Director: Jeff Shelstad
Product Development Manager: Ashley Santora
Editorial Assistant: Stephanie Kamens
Marketing Manager: Anne Howard
Managing Editor, Production: Renata Butera
Production Editor: Marcela Boos
Permissions Coordinator: Charles Morris
Manufacturing Buyer: Diane Peirano
Design/Composition Manager: Christy Mahon
Cover Art Director: Jayne Conte
Cover Design: Kiwi Design
Composition: Laserwords Private Limited
Full-Service Project Management: Elaine Lattanzi/Bookmasters, Inc.
Printer/Binder: R.R. Donnelley—Harrisonburg
Typeface: Times 10/12

Pearson Education LTD.
Pearson Education Singapore, Pte. Ltd
Pearson Education, Canada, Ltd
Pearson Education–Japan
Pearson Education Australia PTY, Limited
Pearson Education North Asia Ltd
Pearson Educación de Mexico, S.A. de C.V.
Pearson Education Malaysia, Pte. Ltd

10 9 8 7 6 5 4 3 2
ISBN 0-13-145240-1

Contents

Introduction

HOW THIS BOOK CAN HELP YOU

If you are concerned about an upcoming PowerPoint presentation, turn to the relevant part of this book for guidance. For example:

- *Your slide design needs improvement.* What colors should you select? What fonts work best? What other design elements might you add?
- *You need to present numeric data.* How do you create a chart that makes the most sense of those data visually?
- *Most of your slides are bullet lists.* How can you add variety to your slides? How can you create effective bullet slides?
- *You are speaking to a new group of people.* How can you structure your presentation to meet their needs?
- *You want to add multimedia to your presentation.* How can you use photographs, Clip Art, audio, or video to enhance your presentation?
- *Deciding on what should go on your slides takes you a painfully long time.* How can you more quickly create slides from your content?
- *You need to explain how a process works.* How do you create a diagram that captures the concept visually?
- *You are nervous about delivering the presentation.* How can you relax and prepare to deliver a winning presentation?

If you don't have a specific question, but need general guidelines, procedures, and techniques, read through this entire book. For example:

- You would like a framework for structuring your message and creating the slides that complement that message.
- You would like techniques to set up a slide design to use in all of your slides.
- You would like step-by-step instructions for creating effective charts, concept diagrams, and text slides.

If you are taking a professional training course, a college course, a workshop, or a seminar, use this book as a reference.

- You may very well be a good presenter already. You would like, however, to polish and refine your PowerPoint skills by taking a course or seminar.

WHO CAN USE THIS BOOK

This book is written for you if you need to make PowerPoint presentations in a managerial, business, government, or professional context—that is, if you need to achieve results through your PowerPoint presentations. You probably already know these facts:

- *PowerPoint presentations are extremely prevalent and important.* Microsoft estimates that more than 30 million PowerPoint presentations are given each day.
- *Your success is based on your ability to present.* Studies verify that your career advancement is correlated with your ability to communicate well, including making PowerPoint presentations.
- *Communication is increasingly important today.* Recent trends—such as increased globalization, specialization, and the use of technology for presentations—make effective PowerPoint presentations more crucial than ever.

WHY THIS BOOK WAS WRITTEN

Many books about PowerPoint and many others about design research have already been written. But this is the only book that combines both design guidelines (what we call "what to do") and technical expertise (what we call "how to do it").

- *Summaries of design research* explain the latest research about such issues as what fonts are most readable, what charts make the most visual sense, and what templates are the most effective.
- *Clear technical instructions* tell you how to create effective slides in a concise straightforward way that a busy reader can understand quickly.

Between the two of us, we have taught thousands of participants in courses and workshops worldwide. Many of our students and clients have found other books on PowerPoint skills too long and too full of complex, incomprehensible technical details. This book, in contrast, is appropriate for you if you want a guide that is short, professional, and readable.

- *Short:* This book summarizes approaches and techniques culled from thousands of pages of text and research and thousands of hours of watching others present. We have omitted bulky examples, irrelevant feature explanations, and exercises.
- *Professional:* This book includes only that information that professionals will find useful for PowerPoint presentations. You will not find publishing skills, such as using PowerPoint to design newsletters or flyers; packaging skills, such as packaging a PowerPoint presentation for distribution in a commercial product; programming skills, such as writing macros; or entertaining skills, such as creating PowerPoint slides for weddings and celebrations.
- *Readable:* We have tried to make the book as clear and practical as possible. The format makes it easy to read and skim. The tone is direct, matter-of-fact, nontheoretical, and nontechnical.

HOW THIS BOOK IS ORGANIZED

The book is divided into four main parts.

1. Presentation Strategy (Chapters 1 and 2)

Your PowerPoint presentation, no matter how beautifully presented, will not be effective unless you achieve your presentation goal. These two chapters offer tips about strategic issues (such as persuading your audience, organizing your ideas, and deciding what to say) and structural issues (such as designing your overall slide organization and tying your slides together into a coherent presentation).

2. Slide Master Design (Chapters 3, 4, and 5)

This section covers techniques to use for your overall slide design. Chapter 3 offers ideas about choosing the most effective colors to make your slides attractive and comprehensible. Chapter 4 deals with fonts—including what font type, style, and size will allow your audience to read your slides more easily. Chapter 5 covers other design elements that you may want to use to enhance your slides' appearance.

3. Individual Slides (Chapters 6, 7, 8, and 9)

This section gives you specific guidance and instructions for creating individual slides. Chapter 6 deals with creating charts to represent numerical data visually. Chapter 7 covers concept diagrams to show flows, processes, or relationships visually. Chapter 8 describes how to create text slides that do not bore your audience. In Chapter 9, you will learn about adding other graphic and multimedia elements to your slides when you need to do so.

4. Presentation Delivery (Chapters 10 and 11)

We cover nonverbal presentation delivery in two ways. Chapter 10 shows you how to improve your nonverbal skills, relax, and gain confidence. Chapter 11 offers tips specific to the delivery of PowerPoint presentations, including proper setup and use of the equipment and what to do if a technical problem crops up.

Glossaries

The three glossaries cover (1) basic instructions for the PowerPoint novice, (2) PowerPoint terms and shortcuts for the "How To Do It" sections, and (3) design and editing terms for the "What To Do" sections.

ACKNOWLEDGMENTS

We offer grateful acknowledgment to the many people who helped make this book possible.

MM: Many thanks to my many wonderful colleagues; to the hundreds of terrific students I've taught at Dartmouth's Tuck School of Business, Stanford's Graduate School of Business, several international universities, and more than 100 executive programs; to our many reviewers, especially Lynn Russell; to Dave Paradi for remaining steadfastly cheerful and efficient, keeping me going, and putting up with the overwhelming rewrites; and most of all, to my dear friends Karla, Nancy, Fran, Claire, Laurie, and Mary—for being there when I needed them.

DP: Thanks to the many professional speaking colleagues who have helped me discover and develop my expertise and have encouraged me to write, including Dr. Brad McRae, Richard Peterson, Warren Evans, Kit Grant, Linda Tarrant, and my many other colleagues at CAPS and NSA; to all of those who have attended my programs and subscribe to my newsletter, your questions and input have helped refine my ideas and challenged me to deepen my expertise; to Mary Munter, who saw the potential in a former student and worked so hard to make this book happen; to my children Andrew and Laura for letting me work on the book; and, most of all, to my wonderful wife Sheila who was the one who had the idea in the first place.

Finally, we would both like to acknowledge our sources listed in the bibliography.

Mary Munter
Tuck School of Business
Dartmouth College

Dave Paradi
ThinkOutsideTheSlide.com

PART I

Presentation Strategy

CHAPTER OUTLINE

I. STRATEGY: WHAT TO DO
   1. Determine your presentation type and goal.
   2. Analyze your audience.

II. STRUCTURE: WHAT TO DO
   1. Research and collect information.
   2. Organize the information.
   3. Decide what you will say.
   4. Prepare your note cards.

CHAPTER 1

From Strategy to Structure

Many people are so excited about the bells and whistles of PowerPoint that they neglect to think through their presentation strategy and structure. Remember that all the fancy slides in the world will do you no good unless your presentation "works"—that is, unless you achieve your desired outcome.

To achieve that outcome, then, before you even think about slide design, take the time to analyze . . .

- *Your strategy:* Determine your goal and analyze your audience.
- *Your structure:* Research, organize, and decide what you will say.

I. STRATEGY: WHAT TO DO

Always set your strategy before you start your slides.

1. Determine your presentation type and goal.

First, define your presentation type and goal.

What type of presentation are you giving? Most business presentations are either informative or persuasive.

- *Informative presentations:* In informative presentations, your objective is to educate the audience—such as, project updates, financial results reviews, or human resource policy explanations.
- *Persuasive presentations:* In persuasive presentations, you are trying to persuade the audience to take some action— such as, asking someone to purchase a product or service, agree to a course of action, or decide between two alternatives.
- *Combination:* In some situations, you may have a combination presentation, in which the first part is informative and the second part is persuasive.

What is your presentation goal? Your presentation goal should be so clear that you can state it in one sentence: "As a result of this presentation, the audience will know or understand ..." (informative) or "As a result of this presentation, the audience will do . . ." (persuasive).

Examples: informative presentation goals

As a result of this presentation,
... the department will understand the new invoicing procedures.
... my boss will learn the results of our new HR program.
... the sales reps will understand the new product enhancements.

Examples: persuasive presentation goals

As a result of this presentation,
... the potential client will agree to buy our services.
... the board will approve my recommendations.
... at least five people will sign up to interview with my company.

2. Analyze your audience.

Once you know where you want the audience to be at the end of the presentation, you need to figure out where they are right now. The more you can learn about your audiences' demographics, knowledge and beliefs, and preferences, the more likely you will be to achieve your desired goal.

Who will be in your audience? If possible, find out exactly who will be attending the presentation: (1) What organizations/departments do they represent? (2) Where are they from geographically? (3) What organizational position/level do they hold? (4) What decision-making power do they have in the organization? For persuasive presentations, find out about those who have the most influence: the key decision makers with direct power and the opinion leaders with indirect power. Sometimes, you may want to gain allies before the presentation itself.

What is their attitude toward the topic? When you know who will be there, you can analyze their current attitudes.

- *Current position:* Is their current position on your topic positive, negative, or neutral? What do they have to gain or lose? Why might they say "no"?
- *Interest level:* What is their current interest level in your topic? Do they see it as a high or low priority?
- *Current situation:* What else do you know about their current situation and emotional state (e.g., the timing or their morale)?
- *Expectations and style:* What are their expectations and preferences (on style, length, or slides)?
- *Easy or hard:* Will your desired action be easy or hard for them to accept?

How much do they know and need to know? In addition to their attitude and emotional level, think about their level of knowledge and what they need to know.

- *Knowledge level:* What do you perceive as their level of knowledge on this topic? What do they perceive as their level of knowledge?
- *Background information needed:* How much background information do they need?
- *New information needed:* How much new information (e.g., evidence, statistics, data) do they need?

How can you find out about your audience?

- *Past impressions:* If you know your audience already, you might want to think about your past impressions, try to put yourself in their shoes and empathize with them, talk with them before your presentation, have them play devil's advocate, or keep collecting information on them based on their reactions and questions.
- *Interviews:* You can interview (face-to-face or by phone) key audience members or those close to them to find out where they stand on the issues and what is important to them. Make sure that you have written out the questions you want to ask and that you take notes.
- *Surveys:* If you have many participants to analyze, you may want to conduct a survey to discover their current positions and their needs. You can gather large numbers of surveys electronically via email or web-based survey tools. Surveys, however, will usually not allow you to single out the key decision makers, so use interviews instead for those key members of larger audiences.
- *Audits:* Another option is to send your audience an audit in which the audience members rank a series of statements based on level of importance. By understanding what is most important to your audience members, you can decide what issues to address in your presentation. You can easily set up web-based audit tools through an email link.

What are their expectations and preferences?

- *Style preferences:* What, if anything, do they expect in terms of cultural, organizational, or personal style—such as formal or informal, straightforward or indirect, interactive or not interactive, or stringent or flexible timing?
- *Format preferences:* What, if anything, do they prefer in terms of format preferences—such as stand-up presentations with slides or seated presentations with a deck?

What is your credibility? Another aspect of audience analysis involves thinking about your audience's perceptions of you (their belief, confidence, and faith in you)—that is, your credibility. The following aspects of credibility are based on French, Raven, Kotter, and Munter, as cited on pages 184–185.

- *Rank credibility:* Do you have credibility by virtue of your rank? Should you stress it or not with this audience? Can you gain rank credibility by associating yourself with or citing a high-ranking person?

- *Goodwill credibility:* Do you have credibility based on your personal relationship with the audience, your "track record," or your perceived trustworthiness? Should you stress that relationship or track record, offer a balanced evaluation, acknowledge any conflicts of interest, or build your goodwill by emphasizing audience benefits ("what's in it for them")?
- *Expertise credibility:* Even if you do not have a personal relationship with audience members, do you have credibility based on your knowledge or competence? Should you share that expertise, allude to how you gained your expertise, or associate yourself with or cite experts?
- *Image credibility:* Are you in some way attractive to your audience; would they desire to be like you? If so, should you emphasize those attributes they find attractive? If not, should you associate with a high-image person or use nonverbals or language your audience considers dynamic?
- *Common ground credibility:* Do you share common values, ideas, or needs with your audience? Should you stress those shared values, acknowledge similarities with your audience, or tie your message to the common ground?

II. STRUCTURE: WHAT TO DO

Once you have set your presentation strategy, turn to your presentation structure: how to collect information, organize it, decide what you will say, and prepare your note cards.

1. Research and collect information.

Even if you are an expert on or an advocate for your presentation topic, gather the information you know in your head, notes, or files to begin the process. Then use any of the following methods to conduct any additional research you might need.

Published facts or statistics: Citing previously published research lends significant credibility to your assertions. Be sure to cite the publication's name to add source credibility and allow people to check if they want to. Facts or statistics add even more to your message if you include an interpretation of what the fact or statistic means to the audience instead of just stating it.

Your own statistics: If you cannot find any facts or statistics that support a key point, you may want to collect your own by performing original surveys or questionnaires. Many web-based tools allow you to quickly survey a large number of people and compile your own research findings.

Expert opinion: When you cite respected experts in the field, you make a stronger point because you can use their credibility to enhance your message. Experts such as senior executives, authors, or university professors are highly respected by most audiences because they have proven their views in the public arena.

Other sources: Other information sources include financial statements, interviews, the web (although material gathered from the web has no guarantee of being true), data CDs, databases, and so forth.

2. Organize the information.

You don't need to decide exactly what you'll say at this point; we'll cover that task in the next section. For now, focus on your organizational structure only.

Methods for organizing: Once you have gathered enough information, you need to organize it in some way. Here are some options:

- *Sticky notes or index cards:* If you are not sure of how to arrange your points, you might try writing out key points, subpoints, and your points of evidence on a separate sticky note or index card. Then arrange the key points in a horizontal line across a desk or a piece of flipchart paper. Underneath each key point, arrange the relevant subpoints in the order in which you think they should be presented. Under each subpoint insert the relevant evidence. Your page or desk will look something like the following diagram.

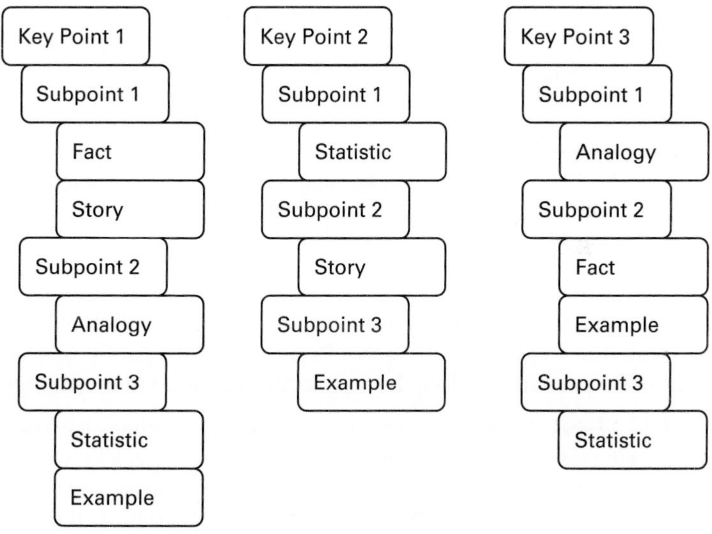

- *Outline mode of PowerPoint:* You can outline your slides by creating (1) an agenda slide that lists your key points, and (2) support slides with explanatory information for each key point on the agenda. In some cases, you will need multiple support slides to back up a point on the agenda.

  The value of using the outline mode instead of entering text directly onto the slides is that when people enter text onto slides, they tend to get distracted by the slide's appearance and start fiddling with colors, fonts, and so on, and lose sight of what is most important: the message.

Note: If you are a PowerPoint novice, please see Glossary 1 for help understanding the following directions.

To access the outline mode:

- In the Outline/Slides Pane, click on the Outline tab.

To compose your first slide:

- Type the title of your first slide → Press Enter.
- Press the Tab key (to indent your entry) → Enter the text of your first point under the title.
- Press the Enter key after each main point you write.

To create new slides:

- Hold down the Shift key and press the Tab key (to move back up to the slide title level of the outline).
- Continue entering the slide title and slide text for each slide in your presentation.

Process for organizing: While you are trying to organize your material, don't expect the process to occur in an orderly lockstep fashion. Be prepared to loop back, to rethink, and to make changes.

- *Take a break:* If you developed your presentation outline all in one working session, you might find it helpful to take a break between developing the outline and testing it. This time-out gives your ideas time to percolate in your mind. By letting the ideas simmer for a day or so, you will come back with a fresh perspective that will make your presentation better.

- *Review your structure:* In your mind or out loud, walk through the points as you have organized them and honestly assess whether each one helps achieve your presentation goal. Talking through your outline with a colleague or associate can be helpful in this process.
- *Revise if necessary:* If you are not sure of your structure's effectiveness, go back and revise the outline. Consider using the sticky note or index card techniques already discussed and start switching points around: Move the beginning to the end or switch the order of some of the key points to see whether they make more sense in a different order. You should not proceed past this point until you are convinced that the outline will enable you to reach your presentation goal.
- *Remember your time limit:* Eventually, you will rehearse your presentation out loud to time it, as explained on page 140, so that you won't run overtime. Instead of waiting until then to think about timing, however, keep in mind that ineffective presenters almost always try to cover too much information. You may discover at this point that you cannot reach your goal in a single presentation. If so, consider revising your goal to fit the structure or revising your structure to fit the goal.

3. Decide what you will say.

Ineffective presenters simply present their ideas in the order that they happen to have occurred to them, sometimes called the "data dump" approach. A data dump may be easy for you, but it is tough on your audience, who then has to wade through your thought process to figure out what you are trying to get at. Instead of a data dump, stand back from all your research and think about what you want your audience to take away from your presentation.

Consider the Audience Memory Curve. The Audience Memory Curve in the following illustration shows what your audience will remember from your presentation, namely what you say at the beginning and the end. Therefore, instead of burying important ideas in the middle of your presentation, state them prominently at the beginning and/or at the end.

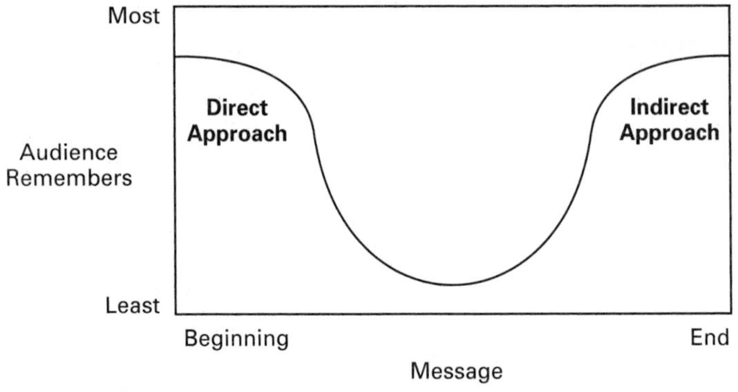

- *Prefer the direct approach:* The direct approach means stating your conclusion at the beginning of your presentation. This approach improves your audiences' comprehension and saves them time because they don't have to figure out where you're going.

  Because of these advantages, you should use the direct approach in almost all business presentations.
- *Use the indirect approach sparingly:* With the indirect approach, in contrast, you save your conclusion for the end of your presentation. Withholding your conclusion until the end is fine for a mystery story, but not for busy business audiences who may resent every minute they spend figuring out what you're trying to say.

Because the indirect approach is harder to follow and takes longer for your audience to understand, use it only when absolutely necessary because of cultural norms, topic sensitivity or emotionality, audience negative bias, or your very low credibility.

Use an effective opening. As you can see from the Audience Memory Curve, your opening is crucial. Given your audience analysis, choose from among the following techniques:

- *Grab their attention:* Use a "grabber" or "hook" to arouse their interest, such as a provocative rhetorical question; a personal story that makes a business point; or a striking image, quotation, or statistic.
- *Show "what's in it for them":* Explain why your topic will benefit them.
- *Introduce your main "take-aways":* Show them what they will learn or what you hope they will do, so that they can listen with these ideas in mind.
- *Build your credibility if necessary:* If your audience doesn't know you, use a technique from pages 6–7 to enhance your credibility, especially establishing a "common ground."
- *Use humor cautiously:* Avoid humor unless it fits your personality, is appropriate and inoffensive for every audience member, and relates to the topic.

Next, give a preview. Always give an explicit preview (a table of contents, an outline, or a road map) of what your presentation will cover. Previews help your audience understand and remember what you say.

Examples of previews

Longer and more formal: I will discuss sales in each of our three regions: the Southeast, the far West, and the Midwest.

Shorter and less formal: I'd like to go over the sales figures in three regions.

State your main points clearly. Your main points need to be organized and easy to follow, much more so than in writing. Readers can look over, slow down, and reread when they wish; listeners simply cannot absorb as much information as readers do. Therefore, remember these three specific techniques that apply to oral presentation structure.

- *Limit your main points.* Do not exceed five to seven major points, because your audience cannot take in as much when listening as they can when reading. Experiments in cognitive psychology show that people cannot easily comprehend more than five to seven main points. Naturally, this doesn't mean that you say five things and sit down; it means that you should group your complex ideas into five to seven major areas.

- *Use strong transitions.* When you are speaking, you need longer, more explicit transitions between major sections or subsections than you do when you are writing. Listeners do not stay oriented as easily as readers do; they may not even remember what it is that you are listing unless you use these longer transitions.

  Ineffective short transition

  Second, . . .

  Effective longer transitions

  The second recommendation is . . .
  Let's move on to the second recommendation.

- *Use backward look/forward look transitions between major sections:* Between each major section or subsection, use a backward look/forward look transition: the backward look repeats what you've just said; the forward look introduces what you will discuss next. Inexperienced speakers may feel awkward repeating themselves so much, but remember, it's better for you to feel redundant than for your audience to feel confused.

  Effective backward look/forward look transition

  Now that we've looked at the three elements of the marketing plan—modifying the promotion program, increasing direct mail, and eliminating the coupon program (**backward look**)—let's turn to the financial implications of that plan (**forward look**).

Keep their interest high. Since the Audience Memory Curve shows that your audience's interest will go down as your presentation progresses, consider the following ways to keep their attention.

- *Include stories,* case illustrations, and examples—not just numbers. Use your own stories so they are personal or use examples you have verified are true.
- *Use analogies* to relate a new topic to something the audience is familiar with (e.g., "Listening to him speak is like listening to nails screeching across a chalkboard.").
- *Incorporate their names* (e.g., "Fatima in accounting and Pat in human resources" instead of "people from different departments").

- *Change your personal energy* (e.g., your tone, pauses, or nonverbal dynamism, as explained in Chapter 10).
- *Ask rhetorical questions* that relate to audience benefits (e.g., "So what does this mean for your business?").
- *Ask for a show of hands* (e.g., "How many of you think our current policy is effective?").
- *Tell them you'll be asking* for their input after the presentation.

Use an effective closing. Your audience is likely to remember your last words, so don't close with a weak ending like "I guess that's about it." Instead, consider these options for effective closings.

- *Give a summary.* One effective closing is to summarize your main points. You may feel as though you're being repetitive, but this kind of reinforcement is extremely effective when you are explaining or instructing.
- *Arouse their enthusiasm.* Another possibility is to close with a quote, an appeal, or a challenge.
- *Refer to the opening.* A third kind of closing is to refer to the rhetorical question, promise, image, or story you used in your opening.
- *End with action steps.* You also might choose to end with a call to action based on what you have presented; make the "what next?" step explicit. In addition, you might remind the audience "what's in it for them" if they take these action steps.
- *Concentrate on main ideas.* If you run out of time, do not try to push through every detail. Instead, concentrate on your main points only, especially your summary slide.

4. Prepare your note cards.

Another aspect of structuring a presentation has to do with the form your notes take. You certainly won't have the time to memorize every presentation you ever make; you will rarely have to read speeches word for word; and you should never simply read your slides aloud word-for-word. Your audience deserves your eye contact and interaction, so instead of memorizing or reading, work from note cards.

Advantages of note cards: With an outline, you will feel more confident knowing that you can refer to your notes if necessary. At the same time, you will be able to avoid both the overreliance on notes caused by word-for-word manuscripts and the terror of speaking with no notes at all.

How to prepare note cards: The purpose of your note cards is to jog your memory; the note card is not a manuscript. You want to spend most of your time during the presentation looking at the audience, not reading. Therefore . . .

- *Do not write out complete sentences.* Instead, use very short phrases for each point or subpoint.
- *Tie your note cards to your slides.* Once you have completed your slides: (1) Print out your slides four-per-page. Then add your notes around the copies of your slides. (This method has the extra advantage of enhancing your eye contact, because you will not be tempted to turn around and read your slides.) (2) Note slide numbers or slide changes on your note cards.
- *Include about five minutes' worth of information* on each card, so you are not constantly changing cards.
- *Use large enough lettering* (either handwritten or printed in a large font) so that you can read your notes at arm's length.
- *Leave enough white space* that your cards are not cluttered or hard to read.
- *Add notes to yourself* (optional), such as "Stand straight!" or "Show line chart here."

Cards versus paper: We suggest using 5×7 or 4×6 inch index cards, rather than 8½×11 inch paper. Think about the following advantages and disadvantages as you choose the method that feels more comfortable and looks less awkward for you.

- *Advantages of note cards:* Notes on index cards (1) are less noticeable to your audience than large pieces of paper; (2) are easier to hold; (3) give you the ability to move around the room instead of being tied to a lectern or desk; (4) allow you to add to, subtract from, or rearrange your material easily; and (5) may help you to use short phrases rather than complete sentences.
- *Advantage of paper:* Some speakers prefer using regular-sized paper for their notes, because they put their paper down on a table, desk, or lectern.

Once you have set your strategy (so you can accomplish your goals) and your structure (so you have organized your content), you are ready to "translate" your structure into slides, as discussed in the next chapter.

CHAPTER OUTLINE

I. STRUCTURE TO SLIDES: WHAT TO DO
   1. Deciding on your key slides
   2. Composing message titles
   3. Tying your slides together

CHAPTER 2

From Structure to Slides

You will save yourself a lot of time if you think through your slide show on the macro (or "big picture") level before you get bogged down in the micro details of composing your slides. So, before you start in on charts and bullet points, think back to the key messages you set forth in your outline (explained on pages 9–11). You need to "translate" this outline into slides. This translation process includes deciding on your key slides, composing message titles for your slides, and tying your slides together.

I. STRUCTURE TO SLIDES: WHAT TO DO

This section includes guidelines for (1) deciding on your key slides, (2) tying your slides together, (3) composing message titles, and (4) using color to reinforce your titles.

1. Deciding on your key slides.

Think about your key slides before you start designing each individual slide. Here is a method for "translating" your structure (opening, preview, main points, and closing, as explained on pages 13–15) into your key slides. We recommend doing this translation on paper or in PowerPoint's outline mode (rather than directly onto your slides) so you will stay focused on your message, not on the slide design.

When deciding on your key slides, however, be sure to actually compose the slides in the following order instead of narrative order: (1) compose your summary slide first, based on your closing or main take-aways; (2) then compose your agenda slide based on your preview; (3) compose your support slides based on your main points; and (4) compose an opening or "grabber" slide, if you wish.

Closing → summary slide: Compose your summary slide first, listing your key take-aways or key ideas. Your summary slide, along with your agenda, is the most important slide in your presentation. So, take the time to make sure it summarizes the key ideas from your presentation and presses them solidly into your viewers' minds.

By composing your summary slide first (before you compose your agenda slide), you can ensure that both your agenda and summary slides reinforce your main messages. For it to be effective, make sure that your summary slide . . .

- *Makes stand-alone sense* of your key ideas (sometimes called "key take-aways") that you want your audience to learn or act on.
- *Ties clearly to your agenda slide,* by being similar (or, better yet, identical) to your agenda wording and visual design.
- *Remains visible* during your question-and-answer session, so that your audience will always have your key ideas reinforced no matter how the discussion goes.

Preview → agenda slide: Your verbal preview (as explained on page 13) should always be reinforced on your agenda slide. This agenda slide serves as your presentation's "table of contents" with the rest of the slides in the presentation like chapters amplifying each idea in this table of contents. Make sure your agenda slide . . .

- *Makes stand-alone sense* of the key ideas you want your audience to take away from the presentation.
- *Ties clearly to your summary slide,* including similar or identical key take-aways, wording, and visual design (such as arrows or T charts, as explained on pages 80–82).

Sometimes the summary slide has more information than the agenda slide, such as an agenda slide with four questions and a summary slide with the "answers" to those questions superimposed on a copy of the agenda slide.

- *Repeats the presentation title in its title,* as shown in the following example, instead of being solely a vague category title like "Agenda," "Preview," or "Presentation Outline."
- *Ties to your support slides* by using the same (or similar) wording for the main points listed on your agenda as you do for the titles of your support slide.

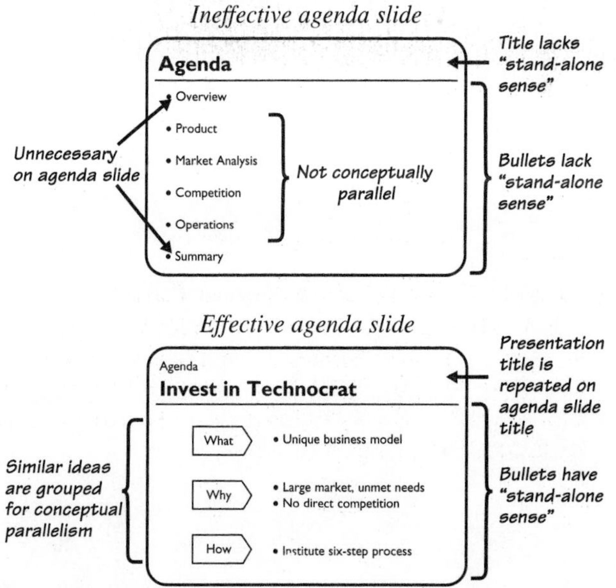

Main points → support slides: Support slides explain, or back up, each point on the agenda. Therefore . . .

- *Prepare one or more support slides* to explain each agenda item.
- *Make sure all of your support slides* follow from, and relate back to, the agenda.

Opening → slide (optional): During your opening, when you are trying to capture your audience's interest (page 13), you do not necessarily need to prepare a special slide. If you choose to do so, you might display any one of the following:

- *A title slide,* reinforcing the subject of the presentation
- *A special opening slide(s)*—such as a striking photograph, rhetorical question, or quotation—to help arouse your audience's interest
- *A black slide* to keep the spotlight on you and your words, rather than on a competing visual (You can create a black slide by drawing a black box over an entire slide; see page 85 for instructions on drawing a rectangle shape.)

2. Composing message titles.

Based on your outline (explained on pages 9–11), you have already turned your key ideas into your agenda slide. Now you will turn your supporting points into "message titles" to put at the top of your back-up slides. A "message title" is the heading or "headline" that summarizes the key take-away of that particular slide.

Compose each title. The message title should make sense to someone reading it for the first time. Put yourself in the shoes of someone who arrived late to your presentation or who missed the presentation altogether and is reading hard copies of your slides. Instead of using a vague, bland title that simply states the subject of the slide, use a message title that reinforces your message. Here are some examples of some ineffective titles, followed by some effective ones.

- *Avoid topic titles.* Ineffective presenters use topic titles—that is, titles that simply state the subject of the slide, but don't tell the viewer what message to take away. (Although you don't use topic titles in informative or persuasion presentations, you would do so in a brainstorming session, when you want to elicit ideas from your audience. For guidelines for running interactive meetings, see *Guide to Meetings,* cited in the biography on page 185.)

  Let's look at an example of an ineffective topic title. As visuals guru Gene Zelazny points out in *Say It with Charts,* given the following slide with a topic title only, your audience might perceive any one of the following messages: (1) the number of contracts has increased, (2) the number of contracts is fluctuating, (3) the number of contracts peaked in August, or (4) the number of contracts declined in two of the last eight months.

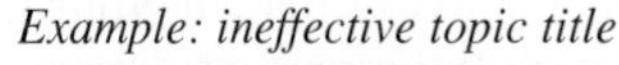
Example: ineffective topic title

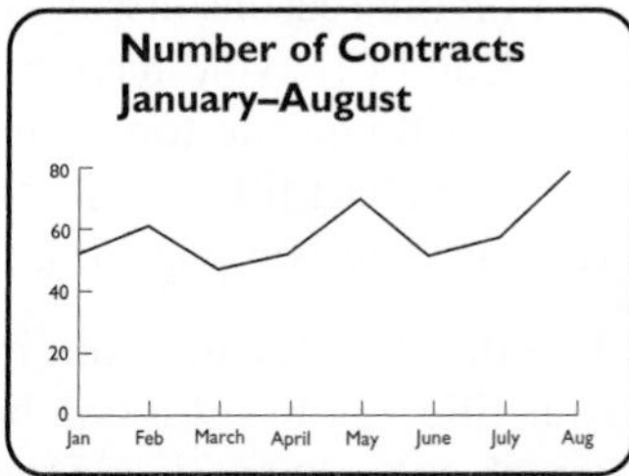

- *Use message titles.* Unlike a topic title, however a message title—that is, a phrase or sentence with a point to it—makes your message clear. Compare the following examples:

Ineffective topics titles:	*Effective message titles:*
Company rankings	Company B ranks second
Use of materials	Product C uses less graphite
Sales over time	Sales declined in March

- *Use message titles in your agenda and summary slides.* Add stand-alone sense to your agenda and summary slides by including your presentation title along with words like "agenda" or "summary."

Consider the benefits of message titles. Message titles offer many important benefits to both you and your audience.

- *Improve audience comprehension:* The audience will understand your visuals better because they see the main point easily.
- *Save processing time:* The audience can also process your visuals more quickly, thus speeding up the information-sharing process.
- *Increase the "stand-alone sense" of your slides:* Message titles have stand-alone sense—that is, they make sense on their own to someone seeing them for the first time. Stand-alone sense is important for audience comprehension, especially for anyone who might tune out of your presentation or come in late.
- *Help you with transitions:* Message titles also can make transitions easier for you, especially if they provide a link from one visual to the next. (See page 14 for more on the wording of oral transitions.)
- *Improve decks (printout of slides) or handouts:* Message titles are will make more sense if your audience is reading them—after the presentation or for the first time—in written form.

Use one title only. Each slide should make one main point, and that main point should be stated in one message title at the top of the slide. Therefore, (1) avoid placing your main message at the bottom of the slide, for all the reasons discussed under the indirect approach (pages 12–13); and (2) avoid having one title on the top of the slide and a second title on the top of an imported chart. In other words, do not enter a chart title on any chart you're going to import from Excel (as illustrated on page 67).

Check your line breaks. (1) Try to avoid having one word all alone on a line in your title. (2) Insert a line break if necessary to keep logical phrases such as "value added" together.

3. Tying your slides together.

Now that you have a big picture of your major slides, think about how to connect your major points visually into a coherent whole. Here are some techniques that can make your slide show coherent:

Consistency: One easy but powerful technique for tying your slides together is to use scrupulous consistency.

- *Same wording:* Use precisely the same wording on your agenda slide as you do on each support slide. For example, if your agenda says "Increase product innovation," your support slide should use that same wording—not similar wording such as "Innovate for new products."
- *Same numbering system:* If the points are numbered in the agenda, use the same numbering system in your back-up slides. For example, if your agenda lays out three main steps for marketing, your support slide for the second step should say "Step 2: Conduct a market survey."

Repeated agenda: Using a repeated agenda slide is another way to remind your audience where you have already been and where you are headed next, especially in a longer presentation. On page 57, we will explain how to duplicate a copy of your agenda slide and insert it each time you move from one main section to the next. Then, pick a method to emphasize the upcoming section, such as . . .

- *Put a box* around the text of the upcoming section.
- *Highlight the text* of the upcoming section in a different color.
- *Insert an arrow* pointing to the upcoming section.

Examples of repeated agendas

Trackers: If your presentation is especially long or complex, consider using "trackers" on each support slide to tie your slides together clearly.

- *What they are:* Trackers serve the same purpose as the "running head" at the top of the pages of this and other books; they remind the audience which section of the presentation you are currently discussing.
- *Where they appear:* As shown in the following examples, trackers usually appear in either the upper-left corner, the lower-right corner, or across the bottom of the slide, where they are visible but not emphatic (e.g., in a smaller font and muted color). Do not use a tracker on the title, agenda, or summary slides.

Tracker
Heading heading heading
- Bullet text bullet text
- Bullet text bullet text
- Bullet text bullet text

Heading heading heading
- Bullet text bullet text
- Bullet text bullet text
- Bullet text bullet text

Tracker

Heading heading heading
- Bullet text bullet text
- Bullet text bullet text
- Bullet text bullet text

Tracker 1 • Tracker 2 • Tracker 3

- *What they look like:* Here are some guidelines for designing your trackers.

  —*Size and color:* Trackers need to be visible, but not call too much attention to themselves. Therefore, use a relatively small size and a muted shade of your text color.

  —*If your agenda consists of words only:* If your agenda is made up of words only (e.g., in bullet or list format), then your tracker should be a shortened version of each main point. In such cases, reduce each main point to one or two words.

—*If your agenda consists of a diagram:* If your agenda is presented as a diagram (such as a pyramid), you might use a mini-version of it as a tracker (as illustrated on page 56). However, never use a diagram for a tracker unless you used a diagram for the agenda.

- *What they include:* Trackers can include either . . .

  —*The current section* that you are discussing at the moment, or

  —*All of the main sections,* with the current point visually highlighted (e.g., in boldface or a different shade).

- *What they do not include:*

  —Do not insert trackers on your title, agenda, or summary slides.

  —Do not include the agenda or summary on your list of trackers; trackers list your main sections only.

For detailed instructions on how to insert trackers, see pages 55–57.

Now that you have decided on the strategy for and content of your slides (in Part I), you are ready to design your Slide Master—colors, fonts, and other design elements—as explained in Part II.

PART II

Slide Master Design

Once you have established your presentation strategy, you are ready to design your slides. Your first task is to design a Slide Master—a master template that will make the colors and fonts automatic and consistent throughout your presentation.

Why should you design a Slide Master when the software has more than 40 design templates available? The reason is that virtually all of the PowerPoint templates are inappropriate for business presentations: they are full of visual distractions (such as graphics, patterns, shimmers, textures, or fades) that make the slides hard to read. Or in the words of PowerPoint critic Edward Tufte, "No matter how beautiful your PP readymade template is, it would be better if there were less of it."

If you must use one of PowerPoint's built-in design templates, consider one of the following templates that are less distracting than others: Blends, Edge, Network, and Pixel. On the other hand, some of the least business-appropriate design templates include: Crayons, Curtain Call, Fireworks, Maple, Mountain Top, and Proposal.

Your Slide Master will be based on the colors, fonts, and other design elements discussed in the following three chapters.

CHAPTER OUTLINE

I. WHAT TO DO
   1. Choose a background color.
   2. Choose a sharply contrasting text color.
   3. Choose an accent color.
   4. Remember other color problems.

II. HOW TO DO IT

CHAPTER 3

Slide Master Colors

You can create hundreds of colors in the PowerPoint software—so just be sure you don't. Do not weaken the power of color by overusing it. Instead, use color to enhance your message, not to decorate your slides. Use color effectively . . .

- *To reinforce your structure:* Viewers sense color relationships clearly and quickly and will stay better attuned to your structure (such as titles versus text) if you use color to emphasize it.
- *In a consistent pattern:* Throughout the presentation, use the same color choices for background, titles, text, bullets, and so forth.
- *For emphasis:* Viewers will look at anything that deviates from your color pattern first, so use color to highlight what you want them to look at.

I. WHAT TO DO

Choose the three basic colors that you will use for all of the slides in any one presentation: (1) background, (2) text, and (3) accent colors.

1. Choose a background color.

First, choose a color to use as the background in all of your slides.

Use a solid color. In the background, avoid patterns, shimmers, textures, or graphics that take up most or all of the slide. In these kinds of backgrounds, the color shade changes from dark to light. When the background color shade changes, text that had good contrast with one shade may be hard to read on the other shade.

Pick a dark cool color or off-white.

- Many designers recommend using a dark, cool color—such as blue, green, or purple—for the slide background because these colors appear to recede, rather than stand out, when viewed on screen.
- Another option is to select an off-white background (like beige, taupe, light sage, light grey/blue, or cream). (See page 39 for exact instructions on how to select these colors.)
- In general, avoid a plain white background because most of the time the white background dominates the slides and viewers are irritated by the glare of a white background in a darkened room. If you are presenting in a bright, well-lit room, however, a white background may not cause glare.

Pick a different color for the slide title area (optional). You might want to choose a different background color for the slide title area (that is, inside the slide title box at the top of your slide). For example, you might choose a blue background color and a darker blue color in the slide title box.

2. Choose a sharply contrasting text color.

Choose a text color that contrasts sharply with your background color. You will use this text color for your titles, text, and sometimes lines.

Pick a contrasting text color. For the best visibility, your back–ground and text colors should contrast sharply. The more contrast these colors have, the easier they will be for audiences to read. In general, this contrast will lead to one of two color schemes:

- A dark background with sharply contrasting light text
- An off-white background with dark text

The chart on the next page includes some effective and ineffective color combinations for background and text colors. (See page 39 for exact instructions on how to select these colors.)

Differentiate text and title (optional). You may want to choose different colors to differentiate your slide titles from the slide text.

Add a line color (optional). If you want to add a line under your title or above your footer, never use a color that stands out, because the line is not an important place toward which you want to draw the audience's eyes. Instead, use black or a muted color with a subtle contrast with the background color.

Check your colors on the big screen or printout. Always check your colors on the big screen or the printed deck. The colors you see on your desktop computer monitor are not the same ones you will see on the large screen or hard copy.

- *Big screen:* Colors almost always look duller on screen than they do on a computer monitor. They may also look different because of the projector bulb brightness or the type of screen. Therefore, be sure to check your color contrast on the screen.
- *Printed deck:* If you are printing your slides to present as a deck, check the colors when printed. Colors vary dramatically from printer to printer and the color on your monitor is different from the color on your printer.

COLOR COMBINATIONS FOR TITLE AND TEXT

Effective color combinations

With these background colors ...	Use these text colors ...
Dark blue, green, purple, or black	White, beige, or yellow
Off-white (beige, taupe, light sage, light grey/blue, or cream)	Black or dark blue, green, or purple

Ineffective color combinations

Colors to avoid	What they are	Why avoid them
Pale colors	Any two pale colors	They look washed out and the lack of contrast makes them hard to read.
Opposing colors	Any colors that oppose one another on the color wheel: red and green, orange and blue, purple and yellow	They clash with each other and seem to vibrate on the screen.
"Crayola" colors	Colors such as lime green or fire engine red	They may look unprofessional.

3. Choose an accent color.

Your background and text colors will set up a pattern that will keep your viewers better attuned to your structure, because they sense patterns of color quickly and subconsciously. Whenever you use a color that deviates from this consistent pattern, your viewers' eyes will be drawn immediately to that accent color.

Select a bright, contrasting accent color. Use accent color sparingly—only when you want to lead your audience's eyes to a particular place for emphasis. Think of your accent color as a spotlight that draws your audience's attention to a certain specific place on your slide. For example, you might want to spotlight a certain column, a certain bar, or a certain piece on a pie chart. Or you could spotlight an arrow to point at a certain place on a diagram.

Tie the accent color to the message title. Use your accent color to emphasize the data that reinforce your message titles, as explained on pages 23–24. Here are some examples to show how.

Accent color used alone

Accent color used with an arrow

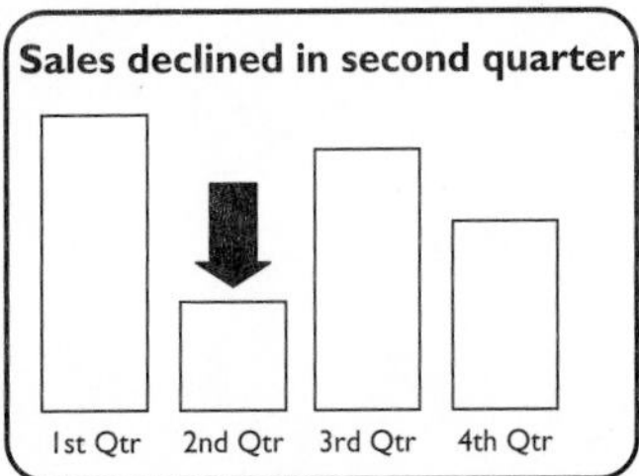

Accent color used with an "exploded pie"

Do not use accent color for unimportant elements. Do not overuse your accent color because you do not want to diminish its effectiveness or to draw your viewers' eyes to trivial items. Therefore, do not use it for unimportant items, such as the line separating the title from the text or the bullet point characters. Instead, reserve the accent color only for those items that are the most important on the slide.

Use your corporate color (optional). If your corporate logo or branding uses a certain color, you might use that color as your accent color on graphs to highlight your results compared to others.

4. Remember other color problems.

Other color issues to keep in mind include the "fruit salad effect," cultural overtones, color blindness, and how your colors look on the large screen.

Avoid the "fruit salad effect." In general, use no more than three colors on a slide (that is, background, text, and accent colors) or you risk creating what design expert Jan White calls the "fruit salad effect"—because the slide looks like the random colors of fruit in a fruit salad. The fruit salad effect is especially prevalent in charts, such as a pie chart with every piece of the pie a different color or a column chart with every column a different color.

Keep in mind the cultural overtones of color. People do not interpret colors in the same way, so all of your viewers will have different associations with color.

- *Cultural associations:* Color associations vary by culture. For example, different colors may be associated with death and funerals: black in some Western cultures, white in some Eastern cultures, and yellow in some Muslim cultures. The colors of a country's flag may also carry certain meanings in that country.
- *Business associations:* Colors may also carry special meanings in the business culture. For example, red may be associated with the phrase "in the red" or green may be linked to money.
- *Company associations:* Color may also have organizational associations. For example, if your company's logo is dark blue, you might want to use this color on a bar chart to distinguish your company from the competitors.

Remember color blindness. Remember also that 5 to 10 percent of your audience is likely to be color blind to some degree and that men tend to be color blind more often than women. Therefore, avoid using green or red as contrasting colors.

Check your colors on the big screen. To repeat ourselves once again, we want to emphasize the importance of checking your colors on a large screen, not just on your computer monitor. All the work you put into designing the consistent look for all your slides on your Slide Master will be wasted if you omit this important step.

II. HOW TO DO IT

Note: If you do not understand any of the following instructions or terms, please see the Glossaries, pages 167–183.

To view the Slide Master:

- Click View → Master → Slide Master.

To set the colors in the Slide Master:

- Click Format → Slide Design.
- Click Color Schemes ❶ → Click Edit Color Schemes . . . ❷.

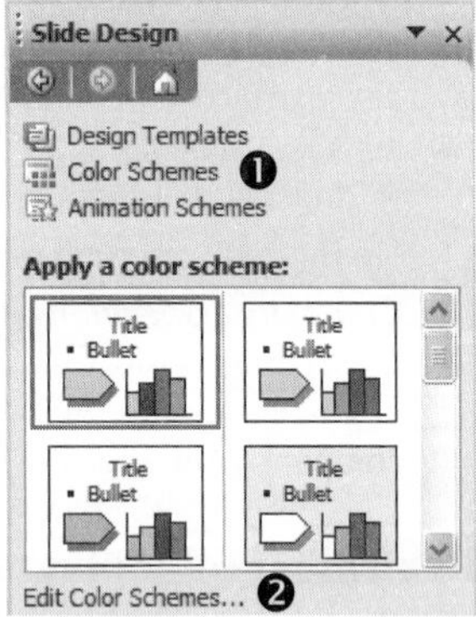

- Click on the Custom tab ❶.
- Click on the color square beside Background ❷ → Click Change Color ❸.

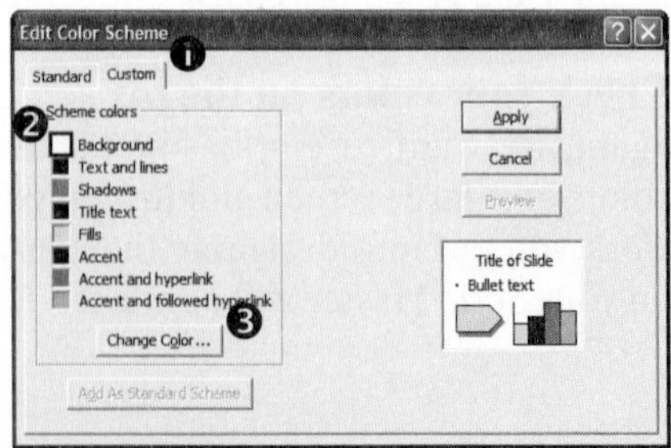

- Click on the color hexagon.

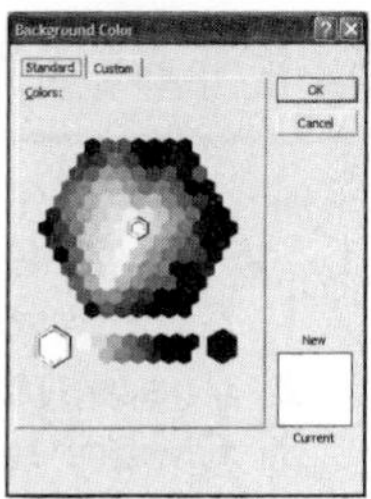

If the colors in the hexagons do not meet your needs:

- Click on the Custom tab → Click on a color series ❶ → Drag the slider bar to fine tune the color within the series ❷ or enter the values for the Red (R), Green (G), and Blue (B) settings → Click OK.

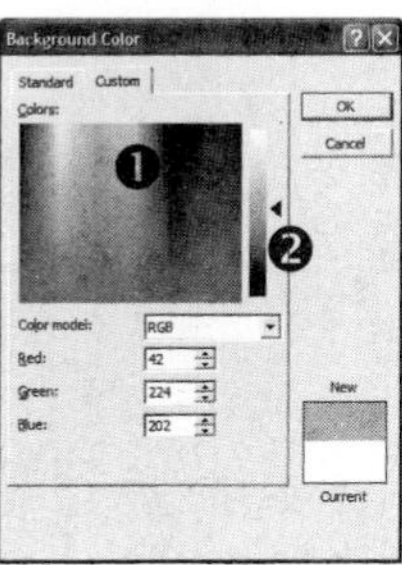

Here are the RGB settings for the colors listed in the table on page 34.

Dark green: R = 0, G = 102, B = 0

Dark blue: R = 0, G = 51, B = 102

Purple: R = 123, G = 15, B = 110

Black: R = 0, G = 0, B = 0

Taupe: R = 227, G = 214, B = 183

Light sage: R = 227, G = 234, B = 183

Beige: R = 227, G = 210, B = 169

Light grey/blue: R = 212, G = 226, B = 226

Cream: R = 255, G = 255, B = 153

White: R = 255, G = 255, B = 255

Yellow: R = 255, G = 255, B = 102

- Click on the color square beside Text and Lines → Click Change Color → Click the color hexagon.
- Click on the color square beside Title Text → Click Change Color → Click the color hexagon.
- Click on the color square beside Accent → Click Change Color → Click the color hexagon.
- Click Apply.

CHAPTER OUTLINE

I. WHAT TO DO
   1. Choose your font, case, and styles.
   2. Choose large enough font sizes.
   3. Choose an unobtrusive bullet character.

II. HOW TO DO IT

CHAPTER 4

Slide Master Fonts

Although PowerPoint may offer you a choice of more than 100 fonts, you will never need to use most of them. Instead, choose your font, case, style, size, and bullet character, always keeping in mind . . .

- Readability
- Consistency
- Unobtrusiveness

I. WHAT TO DO

This section covers how to choose your font, case, styles, and bullet characters.

1. Choose your font, case, and styles.

In general, choose a sans serif font and sentence case, and use font styles (like bold and italics) carefully.

Choose a sans serif font. PowerPoint offers dozens of font choices, but most of them fall into two groups: (1) serif fonts, with "serifs" or "extenders" at the end of each letter stroke (like the one you are reading right now), and (2) sans serif fonts without those serifs, like the fonts on the first two headings on this page (those beginning with a Roman numeral and an Arabic number).

- *Sans serif for slides:* Generally, choose sans serif fonts for your Slide Master because they have the best readability on an electronic display (such as a computer monitor or large screen), since screens have lower display capabilities than paper. Some studies show that Verdana is the most readable font on-screen; Arial is another good choice.

  Examples of sans serif fonts
  Verdana
  Arial

- *Serif for documents:* Reserve the use of serif fonts for printed documents because they have higher resolution.

  Examples of serif fonts
  Times New Roman
  Palatino

Use sentence case for text. From among the following three kinds of "case," choose sentence case (defined below) for extended text.

> AS YOU CAN SEE FROM READING THESE LINES, EXTENDED USE OF UPPERCASE, USING ALL CAPITAL LETTERS, SLOWS DOWN THE READER AND IMPAIRS READABILITY; THEREFORE, USE UPPERCASE SPARINGLY.
>
> Avoid Using Title Case With All Initial Caps Like This For Extended Text Because Title Case Causes Pointless Bumps In The Lines That Slow Down The Reader.
>
> Instead, use sentence case like this, because it shows the shape of each word and is therefore easier to process.

Use font styles sparingly. Do not overuse font styles (such as bold and italics). Instead . . .

- Use font styles sparingly, for emphasis only.
- Never use such styles for extended text.
- Stick to the basics of bold and italics; other styles may impair readability.

Examples of font styles

> **You might choose bold for titles.**
>
> *You might choose italics for subtitles only, but never for extended text like these sentences. Because the letters are slanted and lighter than regular type, they are harder to read for extended text.*

2. Choose large enough font sizes.

One of the most common faults in PowerPoint presentations is that many presenters use font sizes that are too small for the audience to read. Because we usually create our presentations on a computer monitor, we forget that we are not composing a document that will be viewed on a monitor or on paper, but rather a slide that will be seen on a large screen. Also, because we want to jam as much information as possible on each slide, we are tempted to use smaller font sizes.

Once you set your Slide Master with readable font sizes, you will also need to override an annoying feature of PowerPoint that automatically downsizes text to make it fit into the space available. Use the instructions on page 47 to override that default.

General rules of thumb: Here are some general guidelines to keep in mind when selecting your font sizes for projection on screen.

- *Title font:* In general, your title font size should be about 28 to 32 point or larger.
- *Main text font:* Your text font for bullet points and other text should be about 18 to 24 point or larger.
- *Subordinate point fonts:* Your subordinate point font should be at least two to four point sizes smaller than the main text font, or about 18 to 22 point. In general, we recommend against using second- and third-level subordinate levels.
- *Secondary items:* Secondary items—such as axis labels or sources—should be small, yet readable, usually about 16 point.
- *Consistent font sizes:* Once you choose your font sizes, always keep those sizes consistent throughout the presentation. Avoid the temptation to downsize the font occasionally so you can jam more words into the space.

The "8 to 1" rule: Devised by presentation consultant Tom Mucciolo, the "8 to 1" rule is a method by which you can test your fonts' readability when you cannot test on the large screen—by using the ratio of 8:1. Just as you would stand 40 feet away to check readability on a five-foot screen, stand eight feet away from your monitor to check readability on its one-foot screen.

3. Choose an unobtrusive bullet character.

This section covers the design of the bullet characters themselves—such as a filled circle or square—not the text following the bullet point. We recommend that you select . . .

Filled bullet style: The most popular choices are a filled circle, filled square, filled diamond, and arrow. We recommend these filled bullet characters because they are easier for the audience to see.

Examples: filled bullet points	*Ineffective: unfilled bullet points*
●	□
■	○
♦	❑

Slightly smaller size than the font: Select a bullet size slightly smaller than the font of the text so it does not overpower the text itself. Second-level dashes should be slightly smaller than first-level bullet points to visually indicate a sublevel on the slide.

Text color: The bullet itself should always be in your text color, never calling undue attention to itself in your accent or other emphatic color.

Effective spacing between bullet and text: Leave two spaces between the bullet character and the first letter of the text: with less space, the text looks too crowded; with more space, the bullet character seems to float in space, because it's too far from the text.

Hanging indentation: Always use hanging indentation (which is the default in PowerPoint) so that the bullet character "hangs"—or stands out—to the left of the text. With a hanging indentation, second and subsequent lines of text start directly under the text, not under the bullet character.

Effective example: hanging indent

- This example shows how the bullet character "hangs" to the left of the bullet text and the second line starts directly under the text, not the bullet character.

Ineffective example: not a hanging indent

• This bad example shows how the bullet character gets "lost" because the second line starts back at the margin so the bullet doesn't "hang" to the left by itself.

II. HOW TO DO IT

Note: If you do not understand any of the following instructions or terms, please see the Glossaries, pages 167–183.

To view the Slide Master:

- Click View → Master → Slide Master.

To select the title in the Slide Master:

- Click on the text in the Title placeholder box (the box that defines where the title will be on each slide).

To select the body text in the Slide Master:

- Click on the text in the Body Text placeholder box.

To set the font, style, size, or effects:

- Click Format → Font.
- Select the font ❶, font style ❷, font size ❸, and effects ❹.
- Click the Preview button ❺ to see what the changes will look like on the slide.
- Click OK ❻.

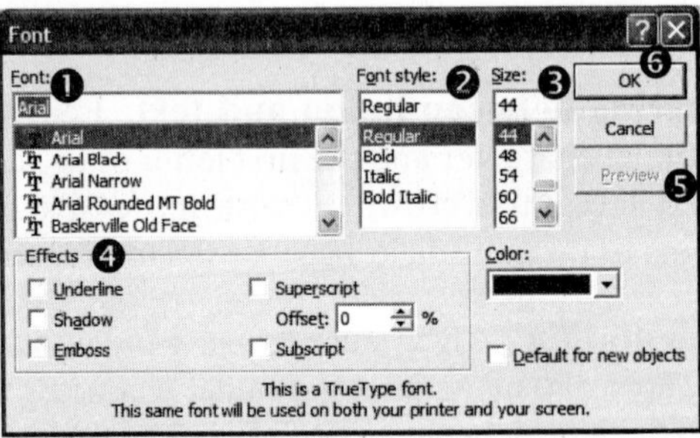

To set text alignment:

- Click Format → Alignment → Select alignment option; virtually always Align Left ❶.

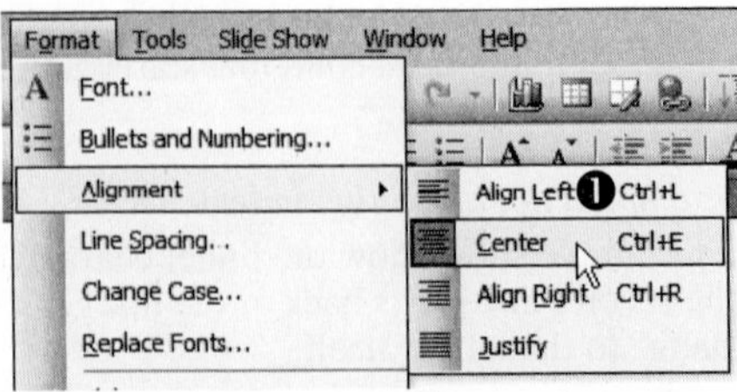

To set a bullet character in body text placeholder:

- Click on level of text in the body text placeholder that you want to set the bullet character for.
- Click Format → Bullets and Numbering.
- Select a filled bullet character ❶.
- Set the bullet size ❷ so it is not too large, usually between 70 and 100% of the text.

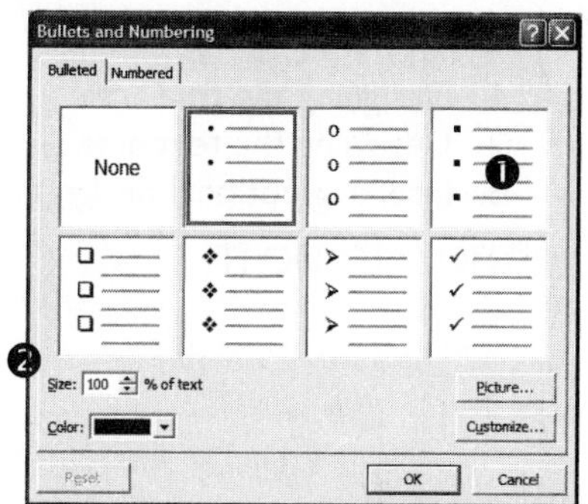

To prevent reduction of font size when typing: You want your font size to remain the same throughout your presentation. However, PowerPoint has the irritating default of automatically downsizing your font to make things fit (e.g., to make a long title fit in the title placeholder). To prevent this automatic downsizing . . .

- Click Tools → AutoCorrect Options.
- Click on the AutoFormat As You Type tab → Clear the checkboxes (the boxes to the left of the words) for AutoFit title text to placeholder ❶ and AutoFit body text to placeholder ❷.

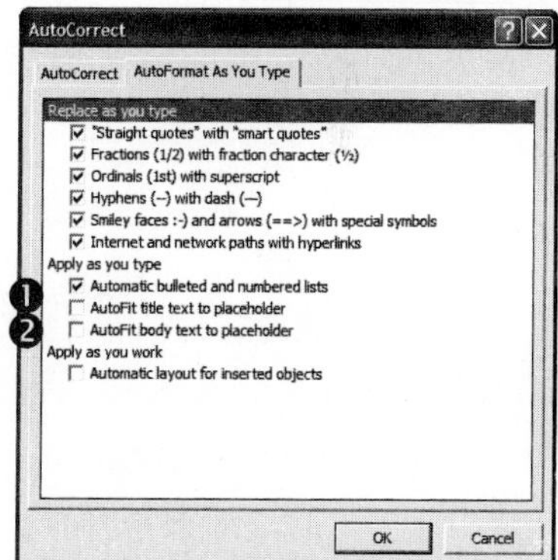

To close the Slide Master:

- In the Slide Master toolbar, click on Close Master View ❶.

CHAPTER OUTLINE

I. WHAT TO DO
   1. Designing the title area
   2. Designing the text area
   3. Inserting optional design elements

II. HOW TO DO IT

CHAPTER 5

Other Design Elements

In addition to selecting your Slide Master colors and fonts, you may want to design the title and text areas and to use optional design elements such as . . .

- Slide transition,
- Lines,
- Company identification,
- Slide numbers, and
- Trackers.

1. WHAT TO DO

This section covers the other design elements contained in the Slide Master design, such as the title area, the body text box, and other optional considerations.

1. Designing the title area.

The title placeholder box is the box (in the dashed-lined area at the top of the Slide Master, as shown on page 54) that defines the appearance of the title on each slide—its location, alignment, and size.

Title placeholder location

- *At the top of the slide:* The slide title should be at the top of the slide, because we read from top to bottom. Avoid placing your main take-away as a "kicker" at the bottom of your slide; based on the reasons explained with the direct approach on page 12.
- *Not crowded against the top:* Don't set the title at the top margin; instead, leave some room above the slide title text so that the color of the background shows above it.

Title alignment: Choose your title alignment based on three options:

- *Aligned left with sentence case:* Most slide titles today (1) are aligned at the left margin (that is, starting each line at the left margin), and (2) use sentence case (that is, capitalizing the first letter of the first word only).
- *Centered with title case:* For a traditional, and some would say old-fashioned look, center your titles and use title case (capitalizing the first letter of each word).
- *Aligned right:* Only occasionally titles are set aligned right to create an unusual style.

Title area sizing: Unless you know you'll have all one-line titles, leave enough room for your title to continue onto a second line.

If your title is longer than two lines, edit it down to two lines maximum; do not add more space in the title area or downsize that particular title font to cram in more words. (See page 47 for instructions on how to override the irritating PowerPoint default that will automatically downsize the font to make it fit into the space available.) Remember, one of the reasons for setting a Slide Master is to make all of your slides consistent, because these consistent patterns are easier for your audience to comprehend quickly.

2. Designing the text area.

Place the main body text placeholder box (in the larger dashed-line area of the Slide Master, as shown on page 54) so that some of the background color shows around all of the sides of the box.

- *Leave some space between the title and body text areas:* Don't place the body text placeholder box too close to the title placeholder box. Space between the body and title text makes it easier for your audience to distinguish between them.
- *Set text aligned left:* The text within the main body text should be aligned left—that is, set so that each line starts at the left margin.
- *Set your text font* at 18 to 24 point or larger, as described in more detail on page 44. In addition, see page 47 for instructions on how to override the PowerPoint default that will automatically downsize the font to make it fit into the space available.
- *Leave some space under the text area:* Don't position the body text placeholder box too close to the bottom border. In many rooms, the bottom of the slide may be hard to see because of the seating arrangement or a low screen height.

3. Inserting optional design elements.

Other design elements include slide transition and a series of optional elements: lines, company identification, slide numbers, and trackers.

Slide transition: "Slide transition" refers to the transition between each slide—that is, how each new slide will appear on the screen. We recommend that you leave the default of "No Transition" so that the new slide simply appears without any unnecessary visual distractions. Avoid other transitions that draw too much attention to themselves and distract or even irritate your audience, such as Comb, Newsflash, Shape Diamond, and Wheel Clockwise.

Lines: You may choose to insert a line on your Slide Master that separates the title at the top and/or the tracker at the bottom of your slide. If so, remember that . . .

- Lines should not draw too much attention to themselves, so choose the same color as the title or text or plain black.
- Lines should be thick enough to be seen, but not so thick that they stand out too much.

Example of slide with separating lines

Heading heading heading

- Bullet text bullet text
- Bullet text bullet text
- Bullet text bullet text

Tracker 1 Tracker 2 Tracker 3

Company identification: Sometimes, you may want to identify your company name, logo, or website on each slide: for example, if you're trying to sell your brand or you know the slides may be printed and pulled apart. Avoid making this information too obtrusive: you don't want your audience to concentrate on your logo design instead of your presentation content.

Slide numbers: Another optional design element consists of inserting a slide number on each slide.

- Do not include slide numbers simply for your own convenience during the design and dress rehearsal stages. Use them only if the numbers will be useful to your audience or to the presentation itself (for example, if you want your audience to be able to refer to slides by number or if you want to be able to jump back and forth between slides).
- Insert slide numbers at the bottom of the slide.
- Use a small font size such as 12 point in your text color so that the audience doesn't really notice that they are there.

Trackers: If you want to use trackers to remind your audience which section you ares currently discussing (as explained on pages 26–27), then you need to . . .

- Leave room for them when designing your Slide Master (as explained on page 55).
- Do not insert a tracker on the title, agenda, or summary slides.

II. HOW TO DO IT

Note: If you do not understand any of the following instructions or terms, please see the Glossaries, pages 167–183.

To view the Slide Master: Click View → Master → Slide Master.

Slide Master

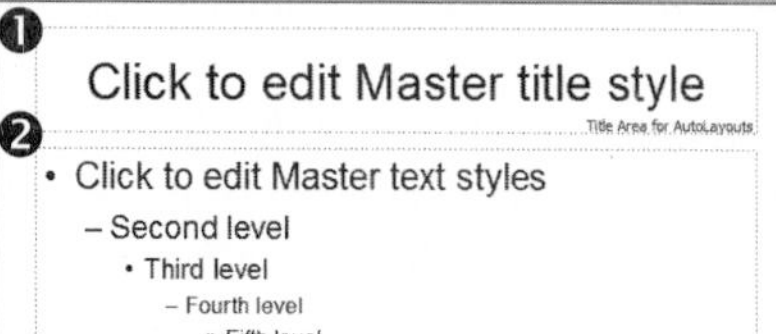

To design the title and text areas:

- Leave space between the top of the slide and the title placeholder (the dashed–line area at the top of the slide) ❶.
- Leave space between the title placeholder and the body text placeholder (the larger dashed-line area) ❷.
- Leave space between the bottom of the body text placeholder and the bottom of the slide ❸.

To insert a logo or other information (optional): You can add your logo or copyright information in the Date ❹, Footer ❺, or Number ❻ area.

- *To insert a logo from a picture file on your computer:* (1) Click Insert → Picture → From File. (2) Select the logo file → Click OK.
- *To make sure the logo does not dominate the slide:* (1) Place it in an unobtrusive location on your slide (usually a corner). (2) Downsize it by clicking on the logo, then use a corner resizing handle (which looks like a white circle) to downsize it. (3) If your logo is very colorful or emphatic, ask your Communications or Graphics department for a version that is either black and white or grayscale, or that has a transparent background.

- *To insert copyright information:* (1) Click in the Date or Footer placeholders at the bottom of the slide, and (2) type the copyright information you want.

To insert slide numbers (optional): You may add slide numbers in the Number placeholder at the bottom right of the Slide Master ❻, (shown on the previous page).

- Click View → Header and Footer.
- On the Slide tab, select the Slide number checkbox Ⓐ to turn on the display of the Number Area in the Slide Master → Click Apply to All.

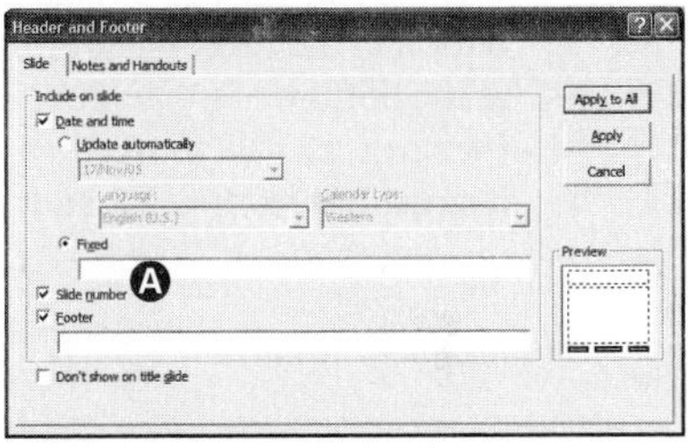

- Click in the Number placeholder on the Slide Master ❻ → Highlight the slide number symbol (looks like <#>) → Click Format → Font.
- Select a 12 point font size and a muted font color.

To insert trackers (optional): See pages 26–27 for an explanation of what trackers are.

- *To insert on individual slides:* Because trackers need to change (based on the section you are currently discussing), you will need to insert your trackers on each individual slide, not in the Slide Master. However, (1) do not insert trackers on your title, agenda, or summary slides, and (2) do not list agenda or summary on your trackers; list your main sections only.
- *To leave room on the Slide Master.* On the Slide Master, however, you need to leave room for the tracker you will later insert on each slide. Therefore, leave the footer placeholder ❺ (shown on the previous page) empty so you can insert your trackers later.
- *To create a tracker composed of words:*

  —(1) Click Insert → Text Box. (2) Click the cursor where the tracker text box should be located. (3) Type the key phrase of each section, separated by four or five spaces between key phrases.

Heading heading heading

- Bullet text bullet text
- Bullet text bullet text
- Bullet text bullet text

Tracker 1 Tracker 2 Tracker 3

—Use a muted shade of your text color for the tracker text.

—Choose as small a font as possible that will still be visible, about 14 to 16 point.

—Choose a way to highlight the tracker that you are discussing in this particular section of the presentation, perhaps in a different color or boldface.

- *To create a tracker composed of a shape:*

—Use the Autoshapes toolbar button in the Drawing toolbar at the bottom of the screen. (See pages 83–88 for further instructions on drawing and moving shapes.)

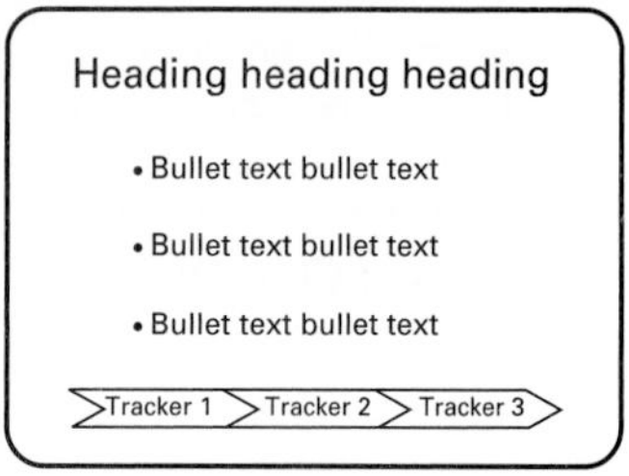

—Add the tracker text to each shape using individual text boxes.

—Click on each shape and drag it so that the shapes are together and they form a single row of connected shapes.

—Use a muted shade of your text color for the text and outline of the chevron, so the tracker does not draw too much attention to itself.

- *To highlight the current section on your tracker:* Change the text color of the current section in the tracker. (See pages 32–36 for details on colors.) Changing its color will make the current section stand out from the other sections. Do not use the text or accent colors because they will draw too much attention away from the rest of the slide.
- *To insert lines under the title and/or over the tracker* (optional):

—On the Drawing toolbar at the bottom of the screen, click on the line toolbar button.

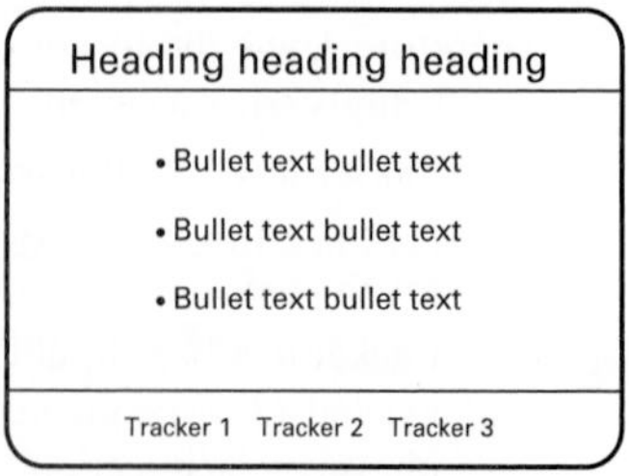

—Position the drawing cursor, which looks like a plus (+) sign, on your slide where you want the line to start → Drag horizontally to the end point of the line → Release the mouse button.

- *To copy trackers to every slide:*
  —Copy the tracker (Click on the first shape → Hold the Ctrl key down and click on the other shapes → Copy the selected shapes → Move to the new slide and Paste the shapes), insert it in the next section, and change the emphasis to this new section.
  —Copy this new version of the tracker to each slide in this section.
  —Optional: You can combine the individual text or shapes in a tracker into a group, which makes it easier to copy to each slide using the instructions on page 89.
  —Repeat the previous two steps for each section in the presentation.

To insert repeated agendas (optional): See page 25 for an explanation of repeated agendas.

- In the Outline/Slides Pane (as shown on page 168), click on your agenda slide.
- Click Edit → Copy
- Still in the Outline/Slides Pane, click in between the two slides where you want the agenda to be inserted. Once you have done so, you will see a horizontal line indicating where the copy will be inserted.
- Click Edit → Paste.
- Repeat as necessary for each time you want your agenda inserted.

To highlight the section you will be discussing next in your presentation, use any of the following options:

- *Use a different color:* Change the font color of the next section's text, following the instructions on page 105.
- *Enclose it in a box:* Draw a rectangular box around the next section's text, following the instructions for drawing a rectangle on page 85.
- *Add an arrow:* Draw a graphic arrow pointing to the next section's text, following the instructions for drawing an AutoShape graphic arrow on page 84.

To close the Slide Master:

- From the Slide Master View toolbar, click on the Close Master View ❶.

PART III

Individual Slides

CHAPTER OUTLINE

I. WHAT TO DO
   1. Select the correct chart type.
   2. Delete chartjunk.

II. HOW TO DO IT
   1. To select a chart type
   2. To delete chartjunk
   3. To import charts from Excel

CHAPTER 6

Charts to Show "How Much"

Many business presentations include quantitative information—such as financial information, marketing projections, or operations analyses. Often these kinds of data will be easier for your audience to comprehend and retain if you show them on a chart (such as a pie chart, bar chart, or line chart) rather than just in words and figures (such as a list, tabular chart, spreadsheet, or financial statement).

Examples: table doesn't show trend; graph does

2005		2006	
January	12,543	January	16,985
February	14,371	February	16,106
March	15,998	March	15,422
April	15,004	April	15,010
May	15,281	May	14,564
June	15,742	June	13,820
July	16,101	July	12,489
August	16,254	August	11,376
September	16,378	September	10,897
October	16,495	October	10,178
November	16,397	November	9,657
December	16,463	December	9,281

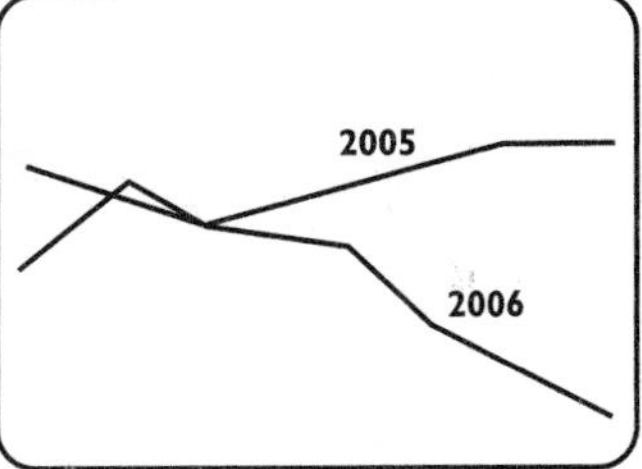

I. WHAT TO DO

To compose quantitative charts, you need to (1) select the correct kind of chart, and (2) delete "chartjunk."

1. Select the correct chart type.

Use the following two tables to select and label your charts.

SELECTING CHARTS	
To show . . .	**Use a chart like this . . .**
Parts of a whole • Components • Percentages • Shares	Pie 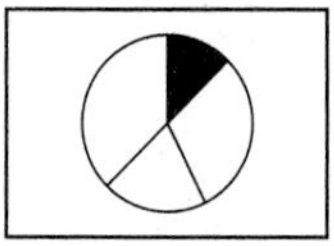 / Exploded Pie 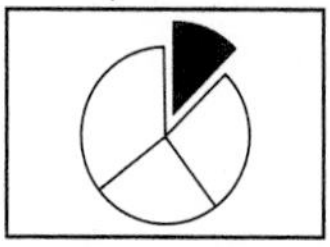
One item compared to others • Rank • More or less than • Difference among	Bar  / Column 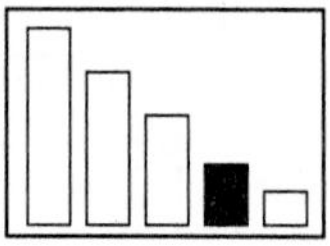
Components of multiple items • Percentages • Shares • Proporations	Subdivided Bar 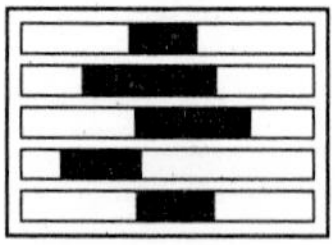 / Subdivided Column 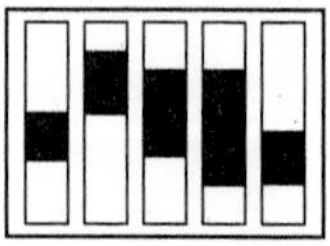
Changes over time or frequency • Increase/decrease • Concentrations • Trends	Line 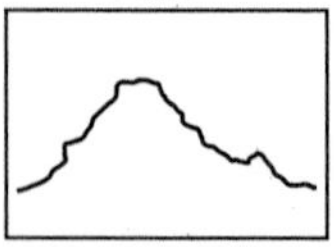 / Column 

Adapted from G. Zelazny

LABELING CHARTS

1. Preferred option:
Label inside section

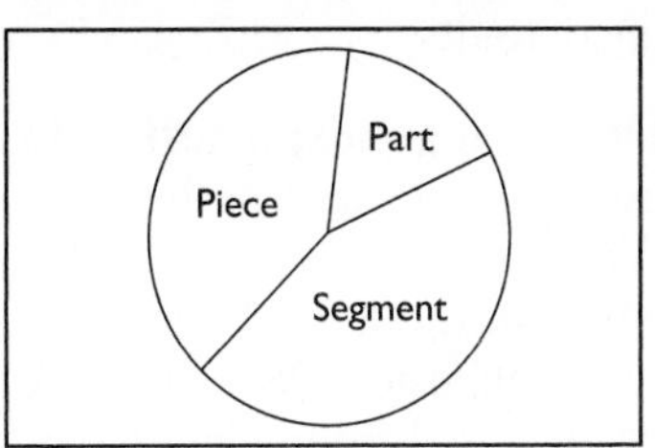

2. Second-best option:
Label just outside section

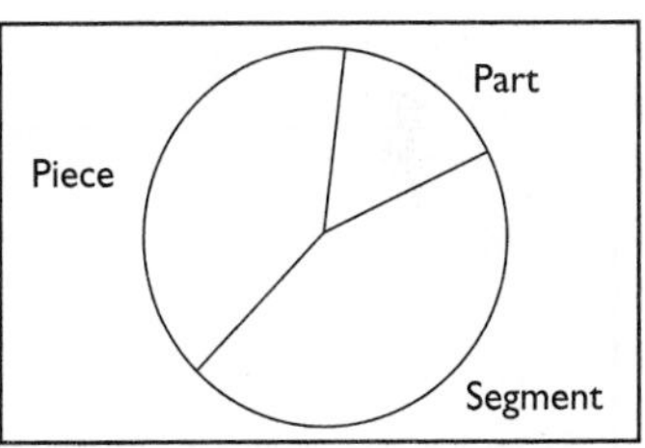

3. Third-best option:
Label and connect to section with line

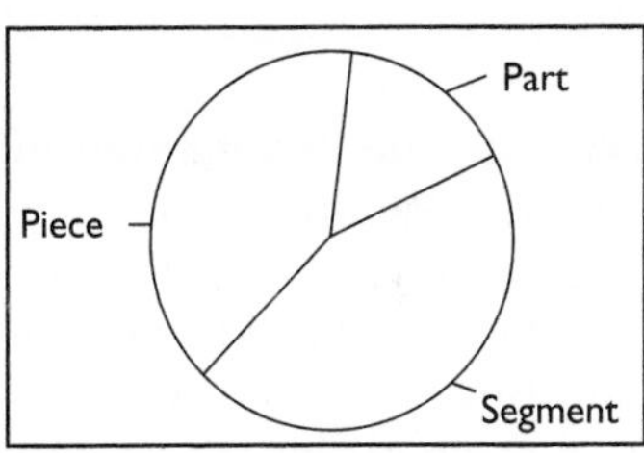

4. Worst option:
Use a legend

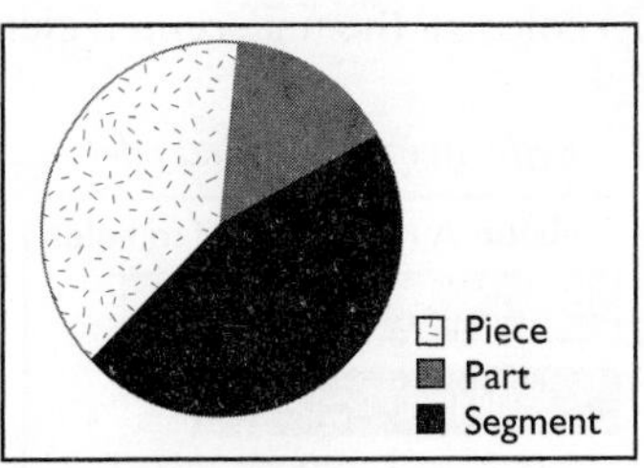

2. Delete chartjunk.

To delete chartjunk, you will have to override the following annoying defaults:

Delete legends; insert data labels. PowerPoint defaults to the use of legends, such as the following ineffective example below at left. When viewers see a legend, they must look repeatedly back and forth between the legend and the chart. Therefore, legends slow down comprehension, distract, and confuse your audience. So delete the legends and insert data labels, as shown in the effective example below at right and as explained on page 71.

Ineffective: legend *Effective: labels*

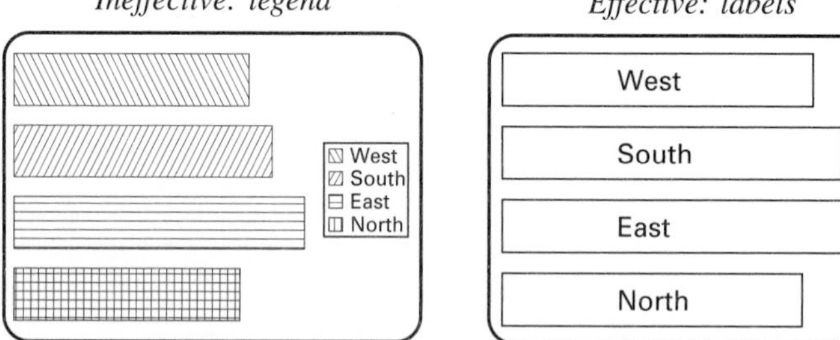

Override the "fruit salad effect." PowerPoint also defaults to overuse of color, sometimes called the fruit salad effect, as discussed on page 37. Random mixes of color are fine in a fruit salad, but in your slides you want to control what gets emphasized. Therefore, you need to (1) override the random default colors; (2) use your accent color on the one element you want to emphasize, based on your message title (as explained on pages 23–24); and (3) color all the unaccented elements the same muted shade.

Ineffective: fruit salad effect

Division A ranked third in sales
Division C
Division D
Division A
Division B

Effective: emphasizes Division A only

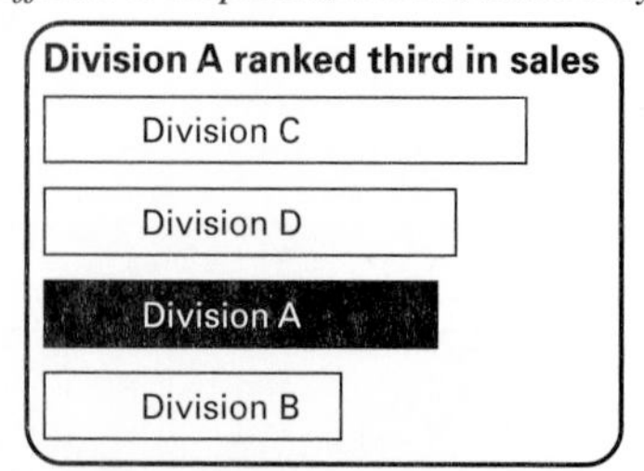

At the same time, remember to keep your colors consistent with (1) the overall Slide Master, so that the chart does not look out of place; (2) your chosen accent color, so that the accent color is the same on all slides; and (3) the contrast between the background color and the text color.

Delete 3-D effects. PowerPoint offers many charts with 3-D effects. Don't use them. Instead, always select a 2-D form of the chart. These 3-D effects not only add unnecessary design elements, but they can also actually confuse and mislead viewers about the data, as shown in the following examples.

Ineffective: 3-D

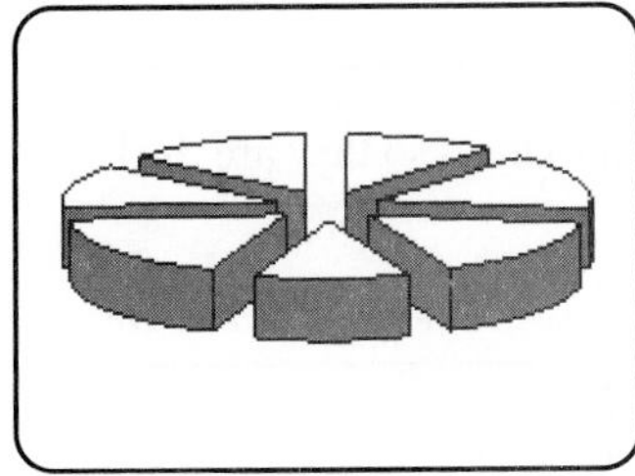

Effective: 2-D

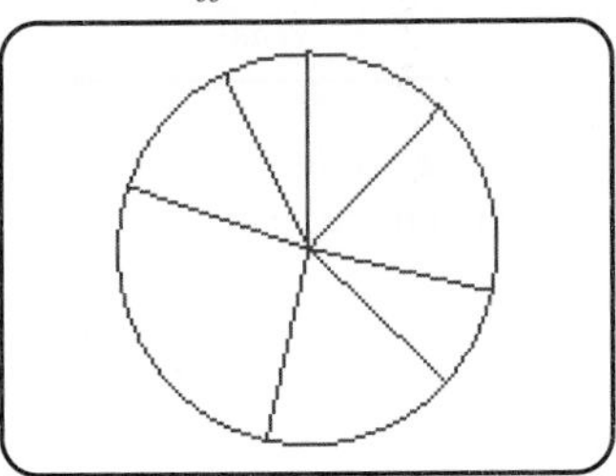

Clean up the lines. The default lines in PowerPoint are full of chartjunk, as you can see in the ineffective example on the left below.

Ineffective: chartjunk

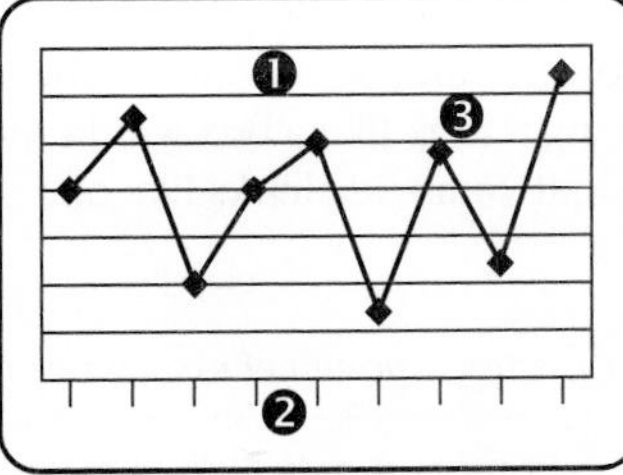

Effective: no chartjunk

- *Remove the following,* all of which clutter up your slide: ❶ unnecessary gridlines, ❷ tick marks, and ❸ data markers. These elements might be useful for printed reports in which you want to show specific values, but in most presentations you want the charts to show general trends that your audience can comprehend quickly.

- *Fix the axis labels.* As shown below, (1) downsize and simplify huge axis labels (e.g., delete all of the unnecessary zeros); (2) remove the axis labels altogether if they are unnecessary (e.g., "Years" or "Months"); (3) consider omitting every other value to decrease clutter or to make the labels readable.

Ineffective: axis labels too emphatic

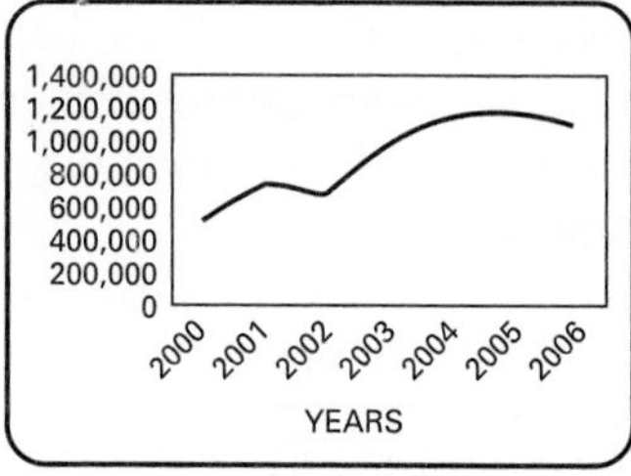

Effective: axis labels unobtrusive

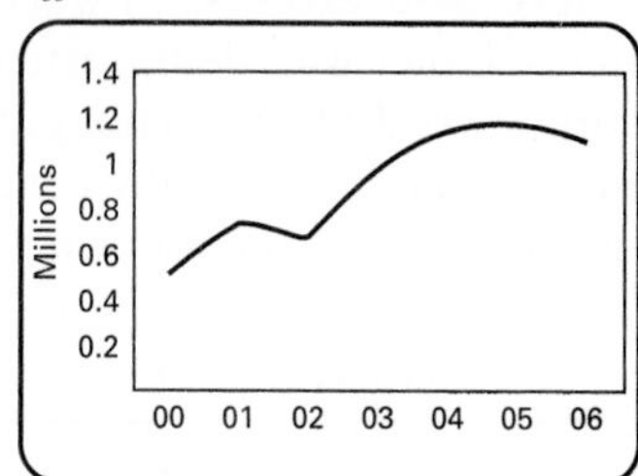

- *Increase boldness of trend lines* on line charts so they are thick enough to be read.

Ineffective: line too thin

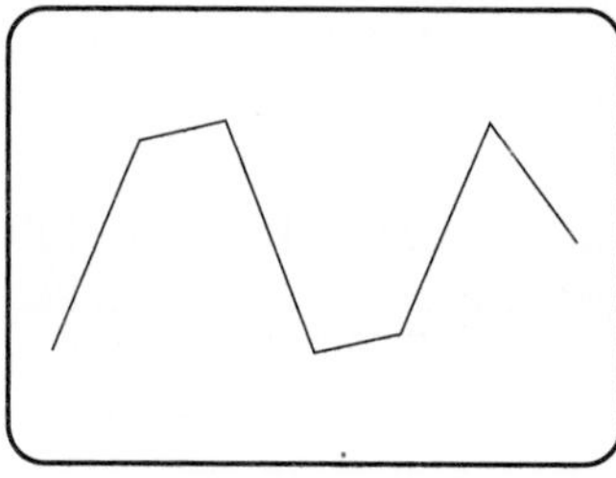

Effective: line clear

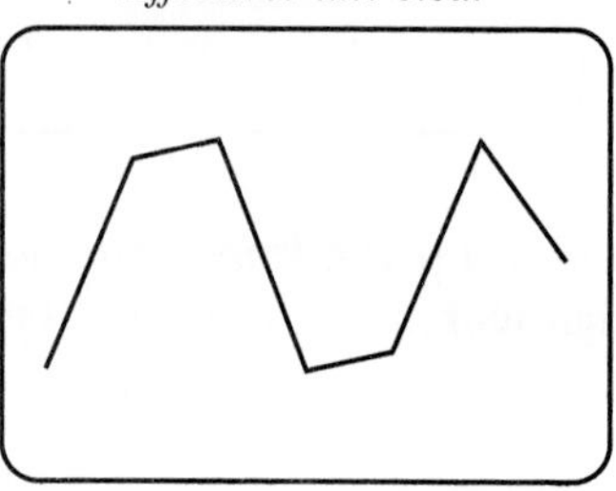

- *Remove unnecessary border lines:* PowerPoint also automatically puts a border around the chart area, making it look like a box within the slide. Remove these border lines so that your slide looks like one coherent whole.

Ineffective: unnecessary chart border

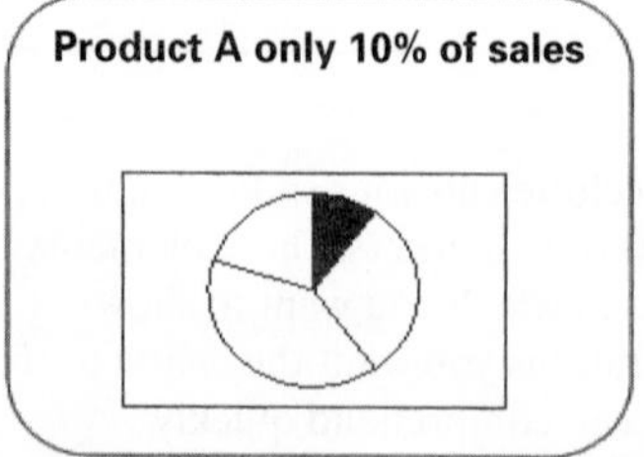

Effective: no unnecessary border

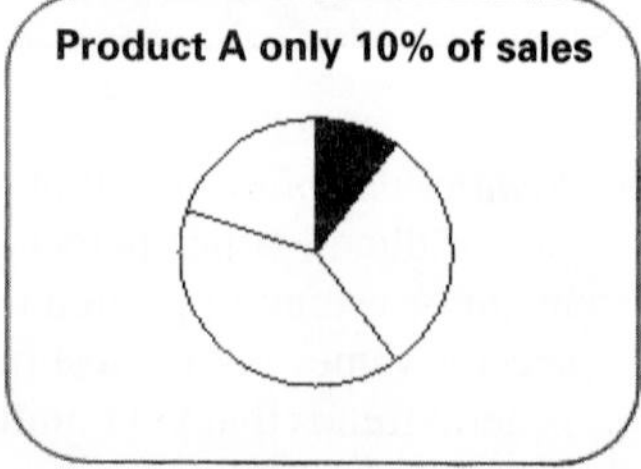

Modify width and spacing. Modify chart elements to fatten up skinny bars and columns and to decrease the space between them. As a design principle, the blank space between each bar or column should be less than the width of each bar or column.

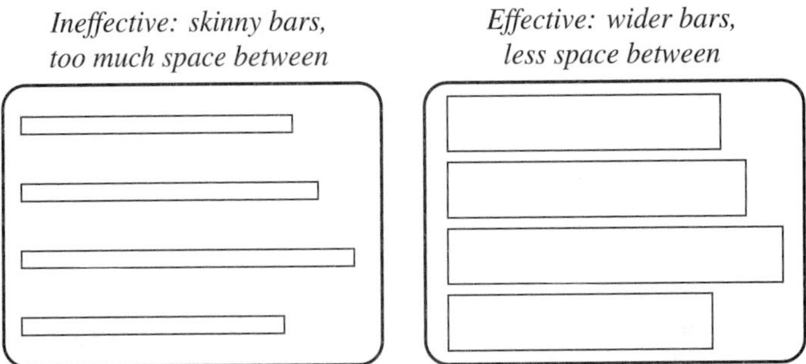

Ineffective: skinny bars, too much space between

Effective: wider bars, less space between

Delete double chart titles. As we discussed on pages 23–24, message titles should appear at the top of your slide. Sometimes, when you insert a chart from Excel or PowerPoint that already has a title, you get a second chart title in the chart area. Delete this second, unnecessary title from the chart.

Ineffective: two titles

Third quarter sales strongest

Quarterly Sales

Effective: one title only

Third quarter sales strongest

Choose your data and its placement on the slide.

- *Insert only the data* you want to include. You don't need to use all the data you have. Instead, select only that data you specifically need for your message.
- *Enter your data* as a "data series" on the datasheet that is displayed when you insert a chart on your slide. Examples of data series include: several companies' percentage of market share (for a pie chart), a rank ordering of survey responses (for a bar chart), or a decrease in profits over time (for a line chart).

Data series

		A	B	C	D	E
		Area A	Area B	Area C	Area D	Area E
1	Sales %	15	10	17	37	18
2						

Resulting pie chart

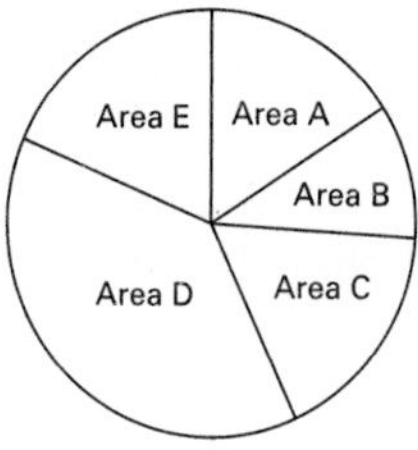

- *Arrange the data in your chosen order* when you are entering it. (1) Don't automatically include all of the data you have. (2) Instead, enter only data that support your message title (as explained on pages 23–24). (3) Don't automatically place the data in some unconsidered order (such as the order in which you received it, alphabetically, or in rank order). (4) Instead, arrange your data in an order that reinforces the point you are trying to make (e.g., best to worst; worst to best; or your company first, followed by the competitors). In the pie chart above, you might want to arrange the pie slices in size order rather than alphabetical order.
- *Restrict and arrange pie slices.* If you are using a pie chart: (1) Try to manipulate your data series so the slide will have no more than seven pie slices, which may require some data to be grouped together. (2) In general, place your most important slice at 12 o'clock by entering it as the first item in your data series; if no slice is more important than the others, arrange the data from smallest to largest.

II. HOW TO DO IT

Note: If you do not understand any of the following instructions or terms, please see the Glossaries, pages 167–183.

The following section covers how to select charts in PowerPoint, delete chartjunk, and import charts from Excel.

1. To select a chart type

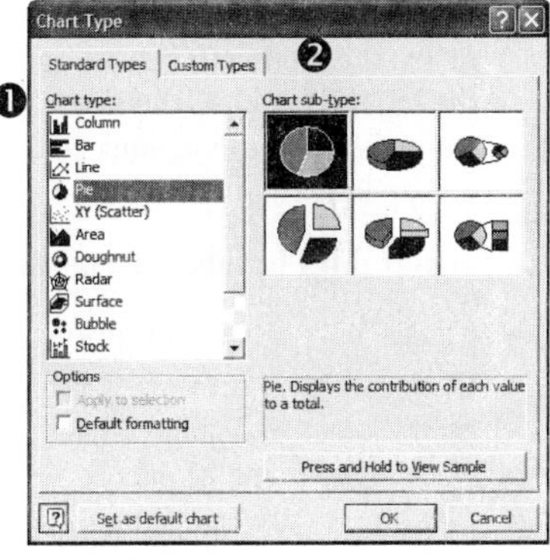

- Click Insert → Chart. (You will see a data table and a sample chart.)
- Click Chart → Chart Type.
- Click on the Chart Type ❶ → Click on any flat, 2-D subtype ❷ → Click OK.
- Click in the data table → Overwrite the existing data.
  —*To delete a data series,* highlight the column or row with the data in it and press the Delete key.
  —*For pie charts,* place the data in the first row of the data table and the data point that you want to emphasize in the first column of the row so it displays in the first pie position.
- Click outside the chart area (i.e., the box that contains the chart).
- After you have cleaned up the chartjunk as described on pages 64–68, click on the chart → Hold the Shift key down and drag a corner handle to make the chart bigger or smaller while maintaining the height/width ratio (also known as the aspect ratio) so it does not look stretched or squeezed.

2. To delete chartjunk

To edit an existing chart: Double-click on the chart.

To delete the chart legend:

- Click Chart → Chart Options.
- Click on the Legend tab ❶ → Click on the Show legend checkbox ❷ to clear the checkmark → Click OK.
- We recommend that you resize the chart after deleting the legend because the size changes when the legend disappears.

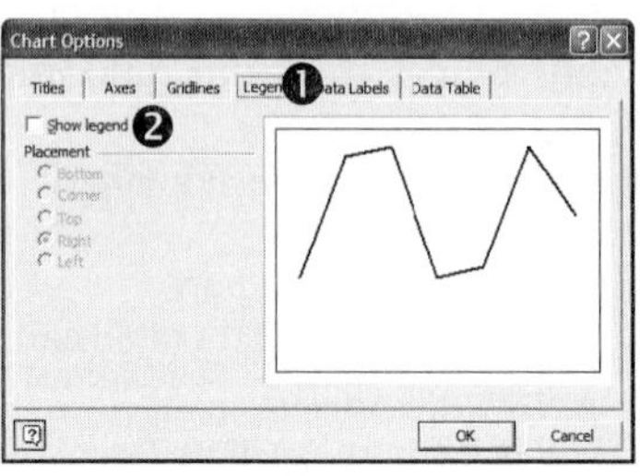

To format data labels (discussed on page 64):

- Click Chart → Chart Options.
- Click on the Data Labels tab ❶ → Select to display Series Name (the name of each row of data in your data table) or Category Name (the name of each column in your data table) as the Label Contents option ❷ → Click OK.

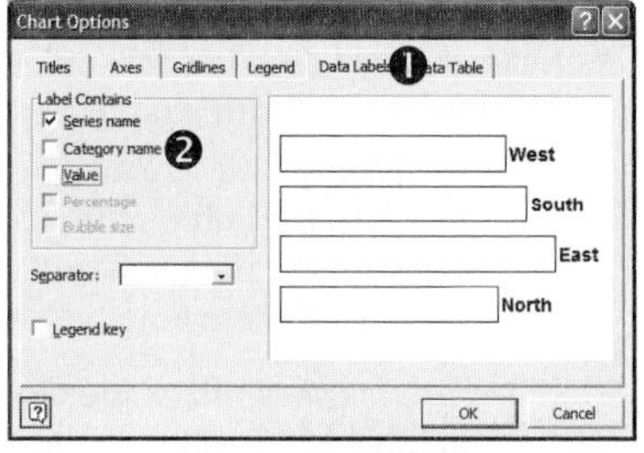

- Right-click on a data label → Click Format Data Labels.
- Click on the Font tab ❶ → Set the font style ❷ and size ❸ (usually at least 14 or 16 point bold font).

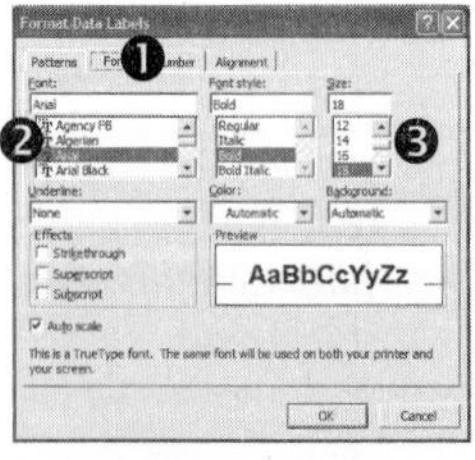

- Click on the Number tab ❶ → Set the format of the data label if necessary ❷. We recommend setting the fewest number of decimal places, given your data.

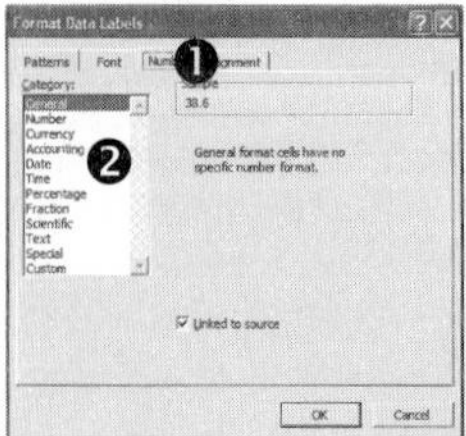

- Click on the Alignment tab ❶ → Set how the label should be horizontally ❷ and vertically ❸ aligned, where the label should be positioned ❹ (the Center option puts the label inside the pie slice/bar/column), and the rotation of the label ❺.
- Click OK.
- To select a single data label: Click on the data label → Right-click the data label → Click Format Data Labels → Follow the preceding instructions to change the font, format, and alignment for just this data label.
- *Optional:* Instead of adding Data Labels, you can add separate text boxes for each label and position them in the bars/columns/pie slices. To add a text box: (1) Click Insert → Text Box. (2) Click the cursor where you want the text to be. (3) Type the text.

To change the appearance of a pie chart:

- Right-click on the pie chart → Click Format Data Series.
- Click on the Patterns tab ❶ → Set the line around each slice ❷ to the automatic black line and set the fill color of each slice to None ❸.

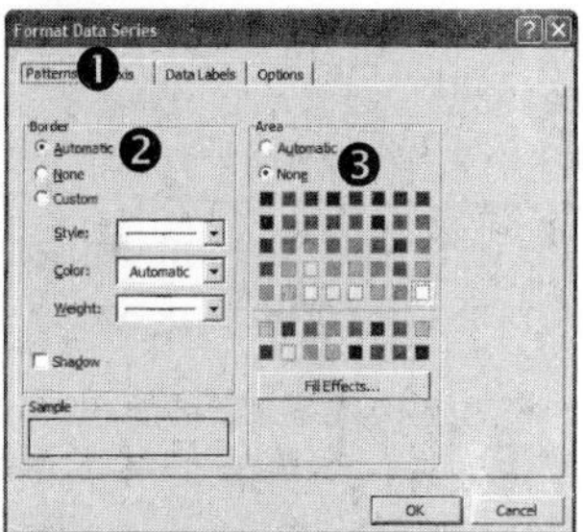

- Click on the Data Labels tab ❶ → Set to display the Value data label ❷ (which will display each value shown on the chart) if you do not want to add explanatory text with separate text boxes.
- Click on the Options tab → Set the starting position of the first pie slice to 0.
- Click OK.

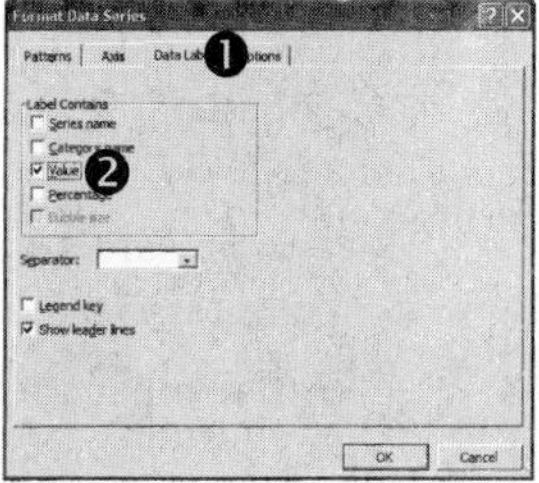

To change the appearance of a pie slice:

- Click on the pie chart → Click on the pie slice → Right-click on the pie slice → Click Format Data Point.
- Click on the Patterns tab ❶ to set the appearance of the pie slices.

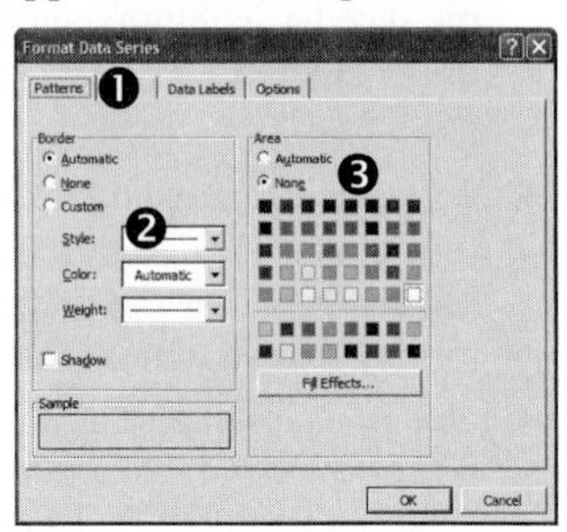

—For all of the slices, set the border to be a line around them ❷.

—For the slice you want to emphasize, use an accent color (as explained on pages 35–36) as the Area fill color ❸.

—For all other slices, use the same muted shade as the Area fill color for all of them ❸.

- Click OK.

To explode a single pie slice for emphasis:

- Click on the pie chart → Click on the pie slice → Drag the pie slice away from the center of the pie.

To change the appearance of columns or bars (including subdivided columns or bars):

- Right-click on one of the columns or bars in the data series (or one of the segments in a subdivided chart) → Click Format Data Series.
- Click on the Patterns tab ❶ to set the appearance of the bars or columns:

—For all of the bars or columns, set the border to be a line around them ❷.

—For the bar or column you want to emphasize, use an accent color (as explained on pages 35–36) as the Area fill color ❸.

—For all other bars or columns, use the same muted shade as the Area fill color for all of them.

- Click on the Options tab ❶ → Set the gap width ❷ smaller to make the bars or columns larger → Check the Series lines checkbox ❸ to add lines between the segments in subdivided charts.
- Click OK.

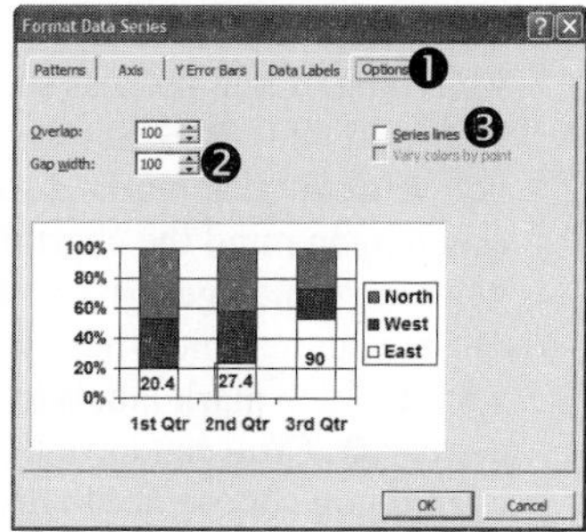

To change the appearance of a single column or bar (or an individual column or bar segment in a subdivided column or bar chart):

- Click on the bar or column chart → Click on the column, bar, or subdivided segment → Right-click the column, bar, or subdivided segment → Click Format Data Point.
- Click on the Patterns tab → Set the appearance of this column, bar, or segment (only the column, bar, or segment you want to emphasize should have a fill color).
- Click OK.

To delete the chart gridlines:

- Click Chart → Chart Options → Gridlines tab.
- Set to not display any gridlines → Click OK.

To change the axes titles:

- Click Chart → Chart Options.
- Click Titles tab → Enter or change the axes titles → Click OK.

To change the chart axes:

- Right-click on the vertical ❶ or horizontal axis ❷ → Click Format Axis.

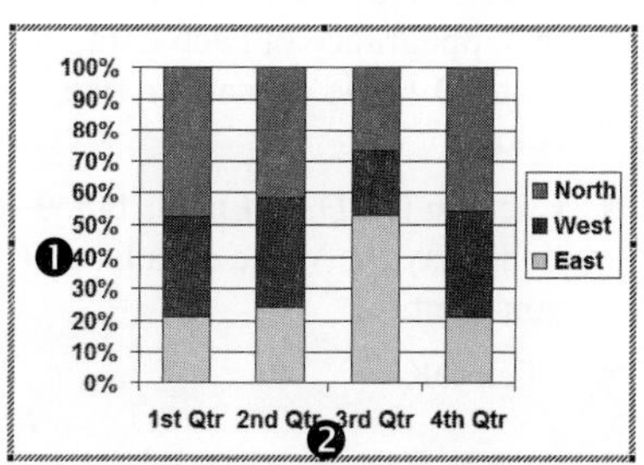

- Click on the Patterns tab ❶ → Set what type of line the axis should be (or no line) ❷ → Set whether you want the tick marks displayed (keeping in mind the chartjunk guidelines on pages 64–68) ❸ → Set whether and where you want the tick mark labels to appear ❹. (You can have labels even if you choose not to display the tick marks themselves.)

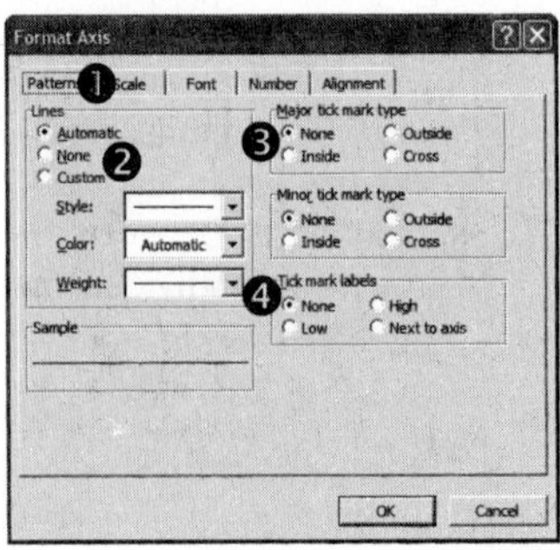

- Click on the Scale tab ❶ → Set the minimum ❷ and maximum ❸ values → Set the Display units ❹ so that the least number of zeros is shown by selecting an appropriate unit (e.g., if the values are in the millions, select Millions as the display units so that the audience sees 1, 2, 3 with the word "Millions" beside the axis).

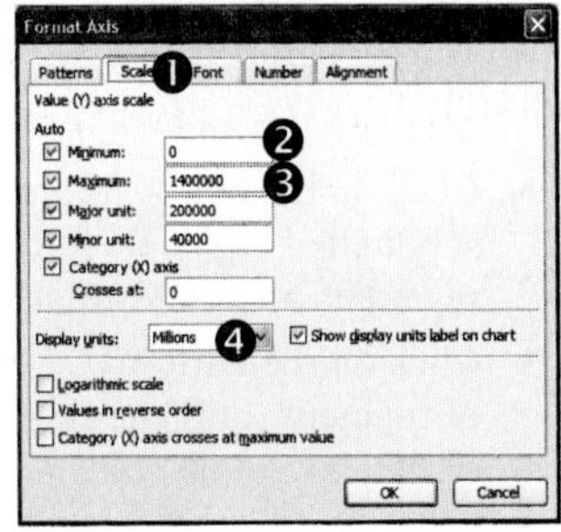

- Click on the Font, Number, and Alignment tabs to set the format of the text for the tick mark labels.
- Click OK.

To change the appearance of a line in a line chart:

- Click on the line chart → Right-click on the line → Click Format Data Series.
- Click on the Patterns tab ❶ → Set the appearance of the line ❷ (color, weight to maximum) and the appearance of each data point ❸ (style of marker, size, color).

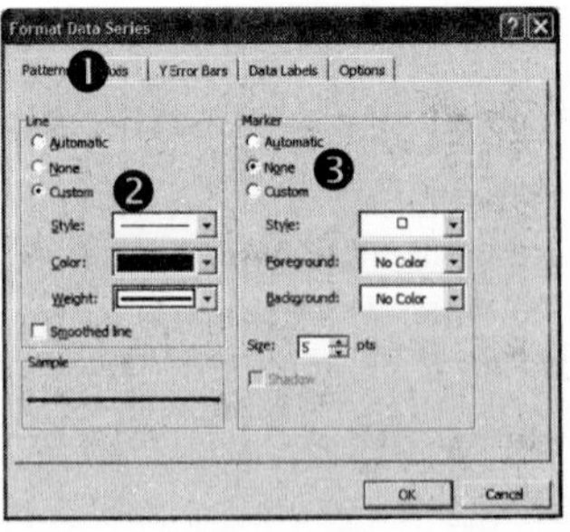

- Click on the Data Labels tab → Set to display the Value data label if you want to.
- Click OK.

To change the chart border:

- Right-click on the plot area (the area within the lines surrounding the chart only) Ⓐ → Click Format Plot Area from the submenu that appears.

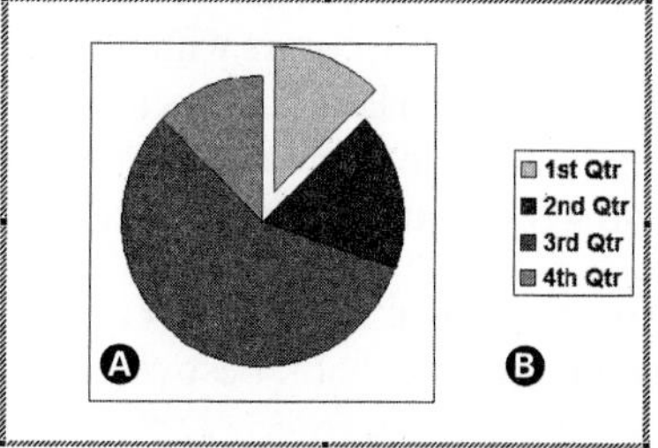

- Select "None" for no border ❶ and no background ❷ → Click OK.

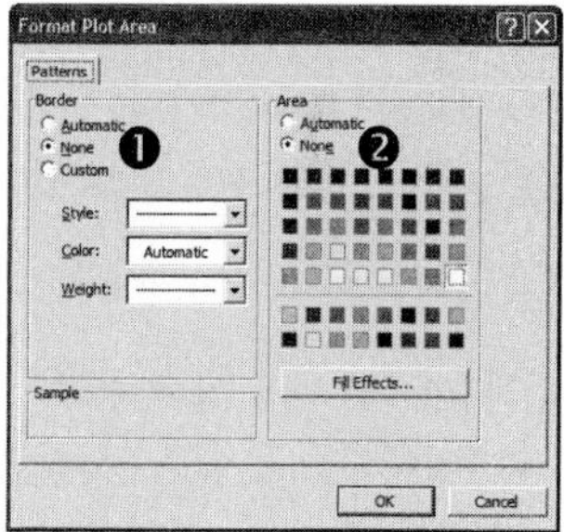

To change the chart area (the area including the chart and legend):

- Right-click on the chart area Ⓑ → Click Format Chart Area from the submenu that appears.

- Select "None" for no border ❶ and no background ❷ → Click OK.

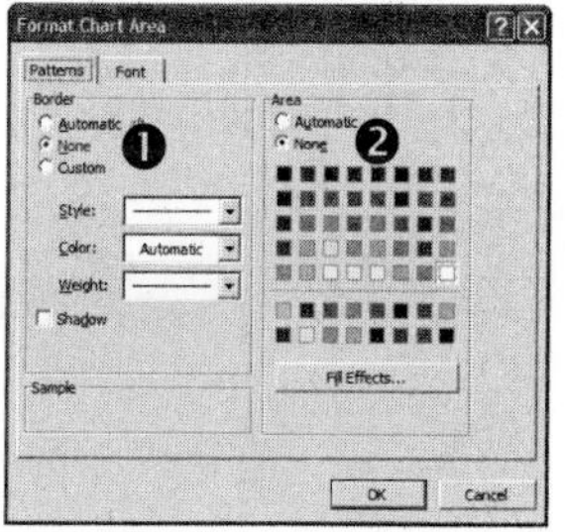

To change the chart title:

- Click Chart → Chart Options.
- Click on the Titles tab → Clear the chart title → Click OK.

3. To import charts from Excel

In general, we recommend creating your charts in PowerPoint because (1) the colors will automatically match your color scheme, and (2) PowerPoint charts are easier to change because you do not need to open Excel to make changes. However, sometimes you will need to create an Excel chart and import it into PowerPoint.

To create the chart in Excel: Use the charting tools in Excel. To make the chart look best when imported into PowerPoint:

- *Do not enter a chart title,* to avoid having double chart titles, as illustrated on page 67.
- *Eliminate chartjunk* using the instructions on pages 70–75.
- *Select chart colors* to match your Slide Master.
- *Clear the default white* chart background in Excel. Once you create your chart in Excel, right-click on the chart → Format Chart Area → From the Patterns tab, set Area Fill to None.

To import the chart into PowerPoint:

- Click on the chart in Excel → Click Edit → Copy.
- Return to PowerPoint.
- Click on the slide to which you want to import the chart.
- Click Edit → Paste Special.

To insert the chart:

- *Option 1: To insert the chart as a single picture object* (so it will not be automatically updated if the source chart in Excel changes): Click on the Paste button ❶ → Click Microsoft Excel Chart Object ❷ → Click OK.

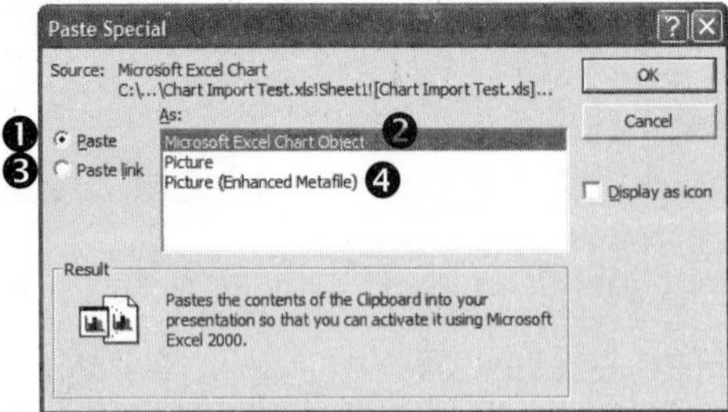

- *Option 2: To insert the chart as a linked picture object* (so it will be automatically updated if the source chart in Excel changes): Click on the Paste link button ❸ → Click Microsoft Excel Chart Object ❷ → Click OK.
- *Option 3: To insert the chart as a picture* whose parts can be separated and modified (PowerPoint will use the Enhanced Metafile graphic format to import the different parts of the chart as graphic objects that can later be broken apart and modified in PowerPoint): Click on the Paste button ❶ → Click Picture (Enhanced Metafile) ❹ → Click OK.

To change the appearance of a linked chart:

- Use Option 2 above to insert the chart on your slide.
- Double click on the chart to edit it in Excel.

To change an Enhanced Metafile chart so you can format each shape or text box individually (as explained on pages 86–91):

- Use Option 3 (pages 86–91) to insert the chart on your slide.
- Click on the chart → Click on the Draw button in the Drawing Toolbar Ⓐ.

- From the menu that appears, click Ungroup ❶.

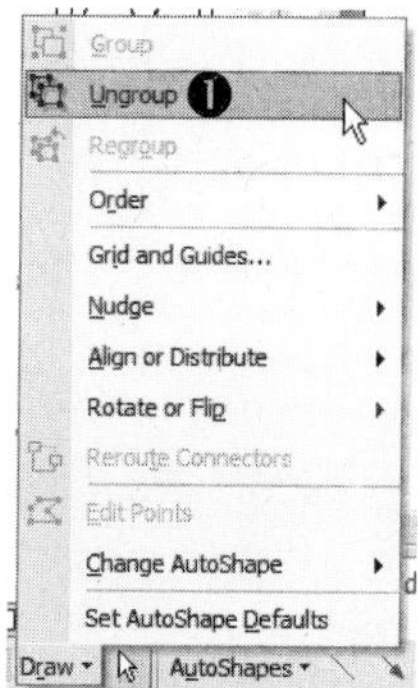

- If it asks you to convert the picture to a Microsoft Office drawing object ❷, click Yes and start this set of steps again.

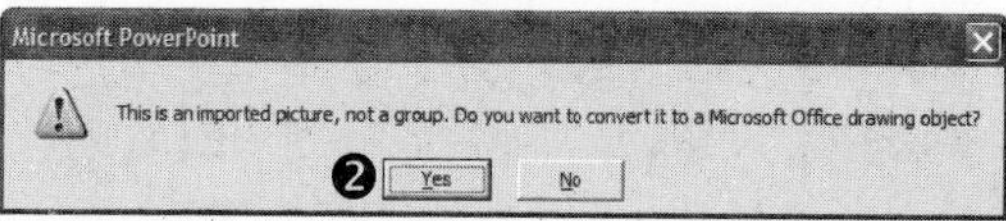

CHAPTER OUTLINE

I. WHAT TO DO
   1. Choose a diagram.
   2. Make sure your diagrams make visual sense.

II. HOW TO DO IT
   1. To create concept diagrams
   2. To modify shapes
   3. To position shapes

CHAPTER 7

Concept Diagrams to Show "How"

Just as charts (such as bar, column, or pie charts) help your audience process quantitative data better than a "data dump" of numbers, concept diagrams (such as matrices, flowcharts, or pyramids) help your audience recall qualitative concepts better than a "word dump" of endless bullet lists.

Concept diagrams add excitement to your slides, prevent you from overusing text slides, and especially appeal to the 40 percent of your audience who are probably visual learners, those who learn better from pictures than from words.

Therefore, most presentations would benefit from using more concept diagrams and fewer text slides.

1. WHAT TO DO

This section covers some popular kinds of concept diagrams and offers some advice on how to make sure your diagrams make sense visually.

1. Choose a diagram.

The following table provides some of the most popular examples of concept diagrams. As you can see, they show ideas for which you could use words—such as "first, second, third"—in a visual format. (For many more such examples, see *Say It With Charts* and *Tools for Facilitating Team Meetings*, both listed in the bibliography on pages 184–185.)

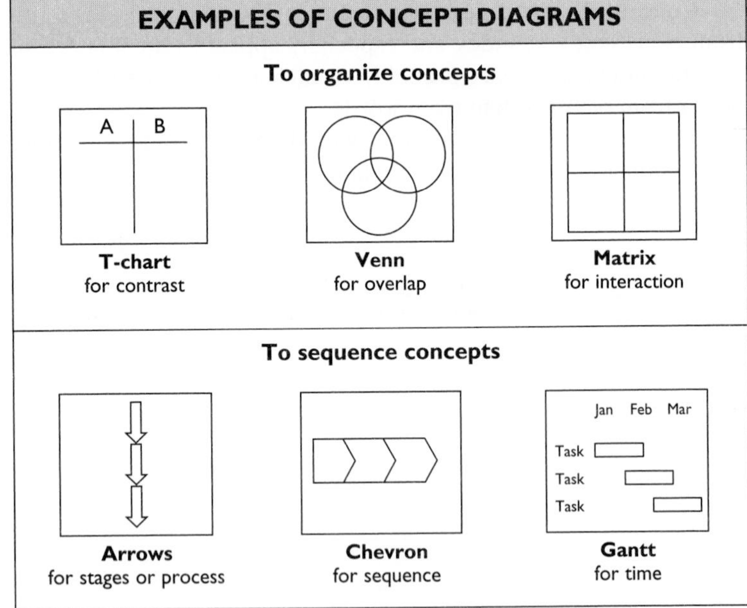

EXAMPLES OF CONCEPT DIAGRAMS

To show process or flow

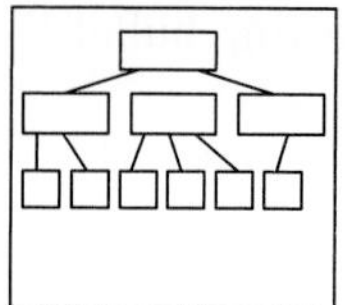

Organization
for hierarchy or flow

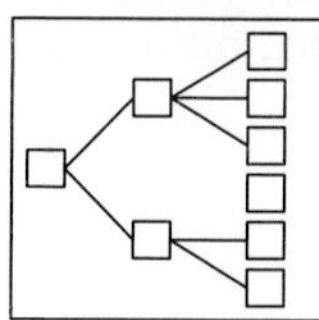

Decision Tree
for decision process

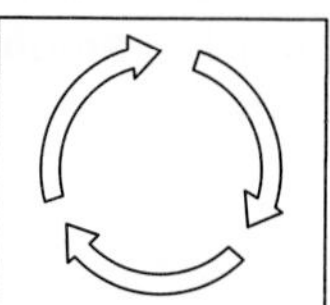

Cycle
for continuous flow

To show relationships

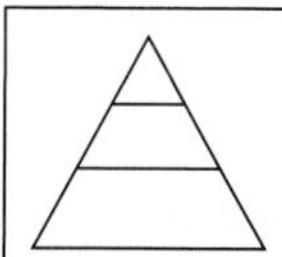

Pyramid
for foundational relationships

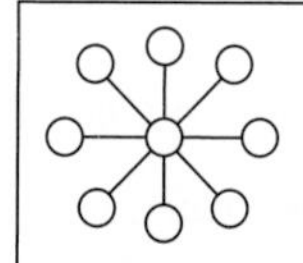

Radial
for relationship among elements

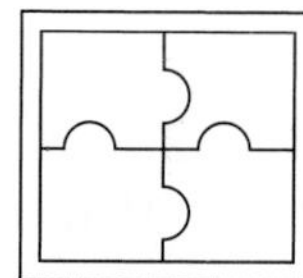

Puzzle
for parts of a whole

Other

Map
for geographical relationships

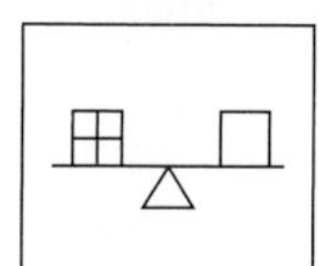

Fulcrum
for leverage or balance

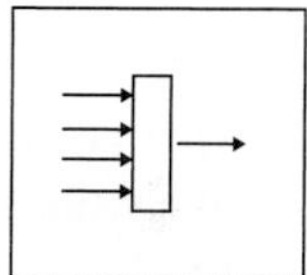

Barrier
for filter, screen, or barrier

Some examples adapted from J. Howell

2. Make sure your diagrams make visual sense.

As we will mention again in Chapter 8, visuals expert Edward Tufte points out (in his diatribe against "death by bullet list") that the relationship among the three points in the following bullet list is unclear:

Bullet list: relationship among points unclear

- Increase market share
- Increase profits
- Increase number of new products

In contrast, the following concept diagrams show three possible relationships among the same three points:

Concept diagrams: relationships are clear

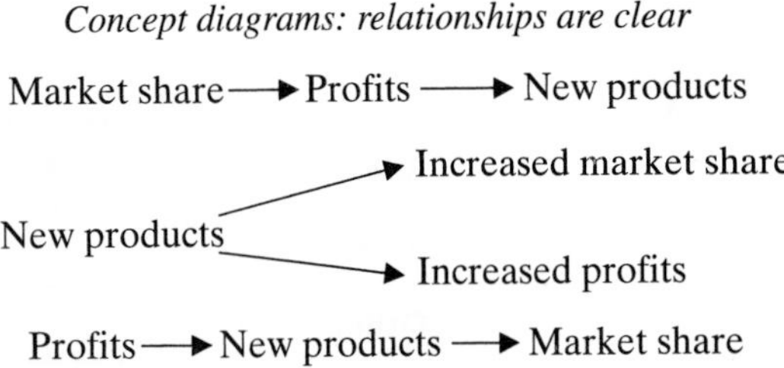

Make sure concept diagrams make visual sense. Your slides won't make visual sense if you just randomly throw in a few diagrams. Therefore . . .

- *Don't use arrows* unless one idea actually leads to the next.
- *Don't use an overlap diagram* unless the concepts actually overlap.
- *Place ideas of equal importance* on the same horizontal level.
- *Group similar ideas* together visually.

II. HOW TO DO IT

Note: If you do not understand any of the following instructions or terms, please see the Glossaries, pages 167–183.

This section covers how to insert or create concept diagrams, and how to modify and position them.

1. To create concept diagrams

To create a concept diagram, you can either use one of the built-in diagrams supplied with the software or create your own diagram using shapes you draw on the slide.

To use built-in options:

- Click Insert → Diagram.
- Click on the diagram type ❶ → Click OK ❷.

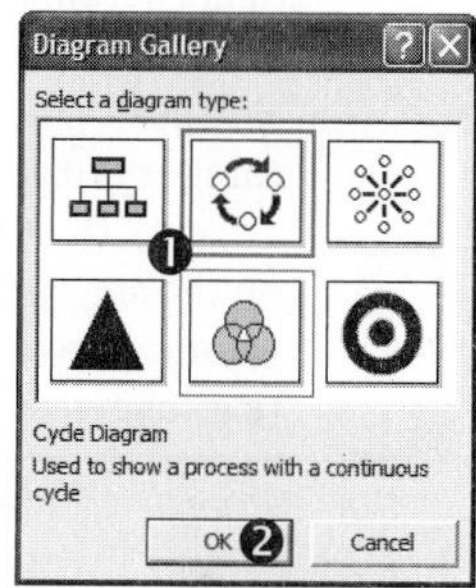

- You will see the Diagram toolbar (across the top of the screen ❶) and the basic diagram of the type you chose.

  Click on an object in the diagram to add text ❷.

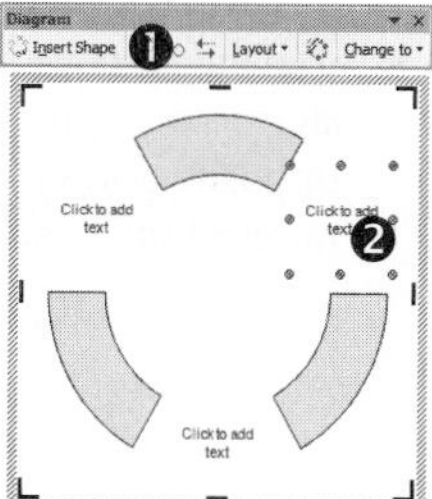

To create your own concept diagram: To create your own concept diagram, use the Drawing toolbar, as shown below. This toolbar is usually displayed at the bottom of the screen. If it is not, Click View → Toolbars → Drawing.

Drawing Toolbar

Note: Your cursor will change into a plus sign (+), known as the "drawing cursor," when you select one of the drawing tools.

- *To draw an AutoShape* (one of the many shapes available in the software, such as those listed in the screen save at right):

  —Click on the AutoShapes toolbar button ❶ (above) → Click on a shape category (e.g., block arrows) Ⓐ → Click on the shape you want to draw (e.g., chevron) Ⓑ.

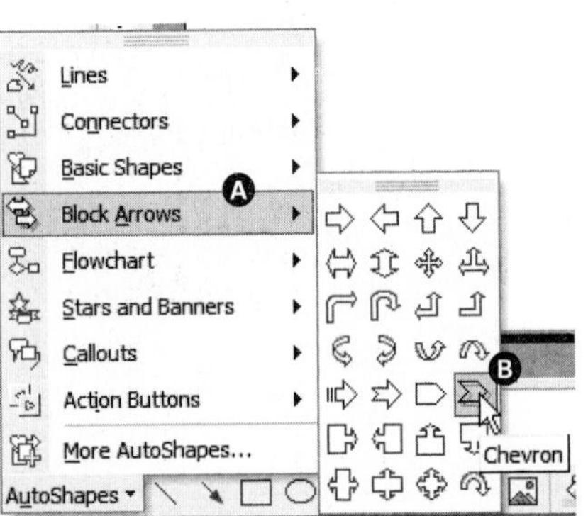

- *To select the shape you want to use,* position the drawing cursor on your slide at one corner of the shape you want Ⓐ → Click and drag to the opposite corner of the shape Ⓑ → Release the mouse button and your shape is drawn on the slide.

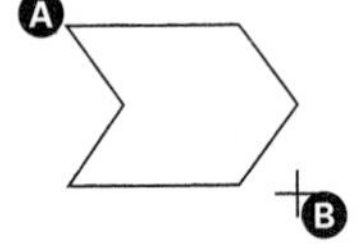

- *To draw a line or arrow:*

  —On the toolbar (shown at left) click on the line ❷ or arrow button ❸.

  —Position the drawing cursor on your slide where you want the line to start Ⓒ → Click and drag to the end point of the line Ⓓ → Release the mouse button.

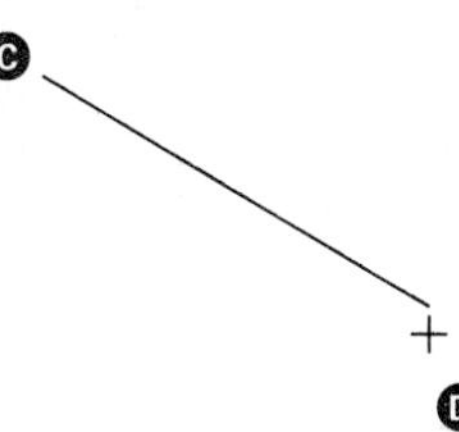

  —*To restrict the line to be drawn at exact 15 degree angle increments* (e.g., 15, 30, 45 degrees, etc.) from the starting point (so you can align connecting lines or shapes more easily), hold the Shift key down as you drag to draw the line.

- *To draw a rectangle or square:*

  —On the toolbar, click on the rectangle toolbar button ❹.

  —Position the drawing cursor at one corner of the rectangle Ⓔ → Click and drag to the opposite corner of the rectangle Ⓕ → Release the mouse button.

  —To draw an exact square, hold the Shift key down as you drag the rectangle.

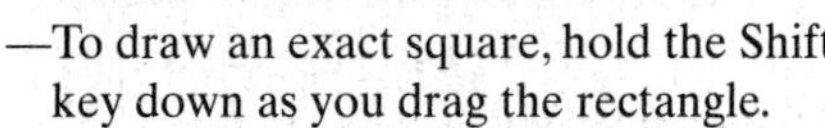

- *To draw an oval or circle:*

  —On the toolbar, click on the oval toolbar button ❺.

  —Position the drawing cursor outside one side of the oval Ⓖ → Click and drag to the opposite side of the oval Ⓗ → Release the mouse button.

  —To draw an exact circle, hold the Shift key down as you drag the oval.

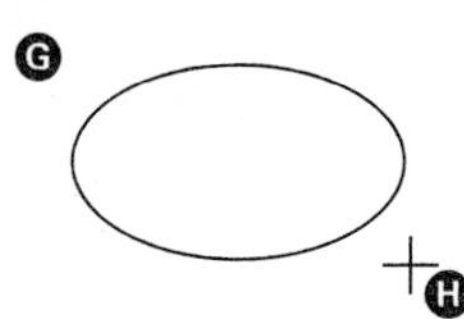

2. To modify shapes

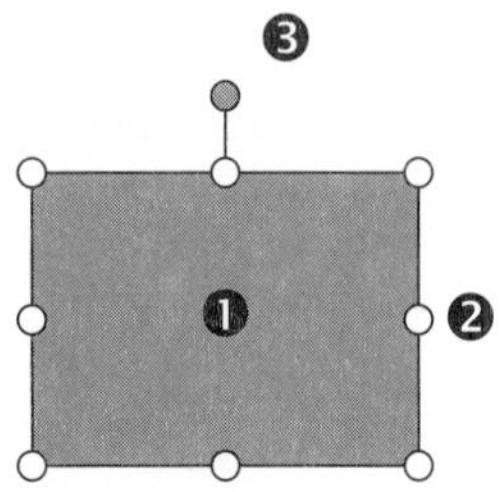

To change the size of any shape:

- Click on the shape ❶ → Click on one of the white circle boundary handles ❷ → Drag the boundary handle to the new size.
- *To keep the same height/width ratio of the shape*: Hold the Shift key down while resizing with a corner handle.

To rotate any shape:

- Click on the shape → Click on the green rotation handle above the shape ❸ → Drag the handle to rotate the shape to the desired spot.

- *To rotate in exact 15-degree increments* so the shape aligns with others: Hold the Shift key down while rotating.

To change the appearance of any object:

- Right-click the shape → Click Format AutoShape on the submenu that appears.
- Change options on the tabs in the dialog box ❶ to set the fill color for solid objects, line size and color, and arrowhead shape and size.

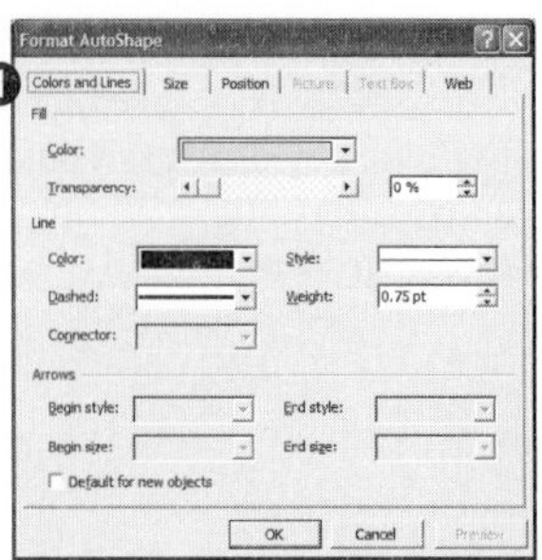

To add text:

- Click on the text icon ❶ in the Drawing Toolbar.

Drawing Toolbar

- Click in a shape to add text to the shape → Type in the desired text.
- Click anywhere on the slide to add another text box → Type in the desired text.
- To downsize the text: Highlight the text → Select a smaller font.

To animate a shape so that the slide builds, letting you systematically disclose one part at a time:

- Click Slide Show → Custom Animation.
- Click on the shape → Click Add Effect ❶ → From the drop-down menu that will appear, Click Entrance ❷ → From the side-menu that will appear, Click Appear ❸ .

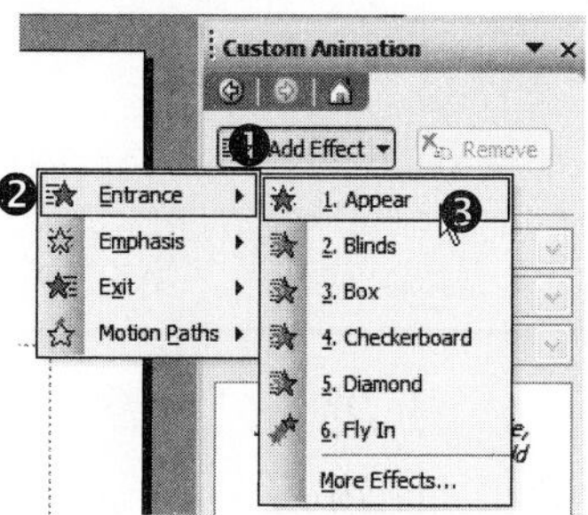

To change the animation order of shapes:

- Click on the element in the list ❶ → Click on the Re-Order button ❷.

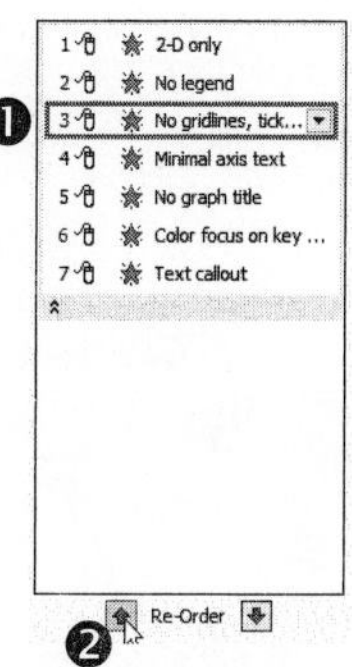

To remove the animation of a shape:

- Click on the shape in the animation list → Click Remove ❶.

3. To position shapes

To save a lot of time when positioning shapes, use the grouping and alignment tools found under Draw Ⓐ on the Drawing toolbar. The Drawing toolbar is usually found at the bottom of the screen, but if it is not there, Click View → Toolbars → Drawing to display it.

Drawing Toolbar

To group shapes together: If you want to copy, resize, or move a number of shapes all together, you can save time by creating a group of the shapes instead of working with each individual shape. The group acts as a single shape and is easier and quicker to work with than each shape would be individually. This grouping is especially helpful if you (1) used a number of shapes together and now you want to copy the entire grouping, or (2) want to make the grouping smaller to fit a certain spot on the slide.

- On the slide, click any one of the shapes → Hold the Ctrl key down while you click on the other shapes you want to group → Release the Ctrl key.
- On the Drawing toolbar shown above, click on the Draw button Ⓐ → From the sub-menu that appears, click on Group ❶.

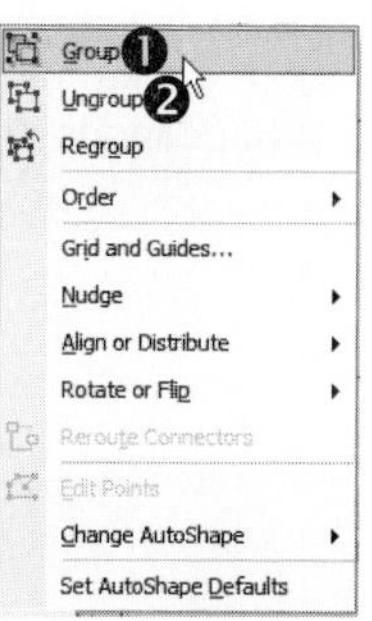

To ungroup the shapes: Click on the group of shapes → Click on the Draw button → Click on Ungroup ❷.

To align shapes with one another:

- Click on the first shape → Hold the Ctrl key down while you click on the other shapes you want to align → Release the Ctrl key.

- On the Drawing toolbar, click on the Draw button Ⓐ → Click on Align or Distribute ❶ → Click on the horizontal or vertical alignment you want ❷.

To align shapes on the slide: Here is an easy way to position two or more shapes evenly on the slide, either horizontally (from left to right) or vertically (from top to bottom) (referred to as "distributing the shapes"):

- Click on the first shape → Hold the Ctrl key down while you click on the other shapes you want to align → Release the Ctrl key.
- On the Drawing toolbar, click on the Draw button Ⓐ → Click on Align or Distribute ❶ → Click on Relative to Slide mode ❷.

- On the Drawing toolbar (shown on the previous page), click on the Draw button Ⓐ → Click on Align or Distribute ❶ → Click on Distribute Horizontally or Distribute Vertically ❷.

To copy shapes from one slide to another:

- *To copy one shape:* Click on the shape → Copy the shape → Move to the new slide and Paste the shape.
- *To copy multiple shapes:* Click on the first shape → Hold the Ctrl key down and click on the other shapes → Copy the shapes → Move to the new slide and Paste the shapes.

To move shapes from one slide to another:

- *To move one shape:* Click on the shape → Cut the shape → Move to the new slide and Paste the shape.
- *To move multiple shapes:* Click on the first shape → Hold the Ctrl key down while you click on the other shapes → Cut the shapes → Move to the new slide and Paste the shapes.

To change the position of a shape:

- Click on the shape → Drag the shape to a new location.
- *To position a shape in an exact location,* move the shape a small distance by holding the Ctrl key down while you use the arrow keys to position it.

CHAPTER OUTLINE

I. WHAT TO DO
   1. Include a variety, not all text slides.
   2. Aim for "six by six," not an overload.
   3. Use "telegram language," not a script.
   4. Control the overall slide design.
   5. Use lettering, not "letterjunk."
   6. Check for correctness.

II. HOW TO DO IT
   1. To compose text slides
   2. To change text format
   3. To import text from Word

CHAPTER 8

Text Slides to Show "Why" or "How"

Virtually all business presentations include text slides—also known as "bullet slides" because they usually include bullet lists—to reinforce the main ideas and structure of the presentation. In fact, text slides are the most common type of slide used in presentations, partly because it is the default layout when you start adding slides.

Text slides can be important tools to keep the audience on track with key phrases that you want them to remember through bullet points. Text slides are also important for displaying accurate quotations that are necessary to review with your audience.

When using text slides, however, keep in mind the following guidelines.

I. WHAT TO DO

This section covers guidelines for avoiding boring and overloaded text slides, one of the banes of ineffective PowerPoint presentations—specifically how to avoid text-only slides, overload, scripts, bad design, and "letterjunk."

1. Include a variety, not all text slides.

Text slides are extremely easy to create, so ineffective presenters overuse them, bombarding their audience with bullet list after bullet list. Overusing text slides undercuts the whole point of having slides—that is, to . . .

- Add interest, variety, and impact
- Increase your audience's comprehension
- Enhance your audience's memory and retention more than with just words
- Improve your interaction with your audience, because you will not just read what's on the screen
- Reach the 40 percent of your audience who are likely to learn with pictures rather than with words

Instead of a barrage of text slides . . .

Use charts and diagrams as well as text slides. Instead of subjecting your audience to what visuals expert Edward Tufte calls "death by bullet lists," caused by all identical-looking slides, make an effort to include other kinds of slides as well—such as charts to show "how much" (pie, bar, column, line, etc., as discussed on pages 69–70) and concept diagrams to show "how" (chevron, cycle, flow, etc., as discussed on pages 80–81).

Don't change your slides too fast. In general, do not show much more than one slide per minute, and use far fewer if your slides are complex. Remember, your audience is seeing them for the first time. If you find yourself with too many text slides per minute, edit them down so you can combine them into fewer slides.

2. Aim for "six by six," not an overload.

In addition to not overusing text slides, don't fill the slides with as many words as you can fit on each slide.

Don't overload your slides. Your audience must be able to comprehend your slides quickly. If you use overloaded slides, they will read the slide instead of listening to you.

Instead of overloaded slides, as author David Peoples suggests, think of your slides as billboards, messages your audience can take in at a glance. Or as design expert Lynn Russell points out, "Just because you *can* fit everything on one slide doesn't mean you *should*."

For example, the following slide does not look inviting and certainly wouldn't sound interesting if you read it to your audience word for word.

Text Visuals Can Hold a Great Deal of Information

- You can put lots of print on a horizontal slide, without wrapping text lines too many times.
- Even if you had 12 bullet points, you *could* fit them all on a single slide.
- You might even decide to change the line spacing to squeeze in your last idea.
- Your font size might still be readable in the back row. But, nevertheless, the slide still has way too many words on it.
- Writing complete sentences means you can read this wonderful prose to your audience.
- If you make margins really narrow and use the space under the bullets, you can squeeze more in, too.

Aim for the "six by six" guideline. As a general rule of thumb, think "six by six"—a maximum of six lines per text slide and an average of six words per line. If you have more than two lines of text in a bullet, either simplify the wording or break it into a main heading plus subpoints. Obviously, you may have to break this guideline sometimes, but don't break it slide after slide and turn your presentation into a group reading session.

Differentiate slides from decks. The "six by six" guideline does not necessarily apply to deck presentations—that is, presentations in which you and your audience all have a hard copy of the slides in front of you as you speak. Decks can accommodate more information because they are read on paper, not on a large screen. However, even if you are using a deck, remember to include white space and to limit the wording as much as you can on each page.

Don't overload animation. Animation is one of the key advantages PowerPoint offers. This tool allows you to "build"—that is, systematically disclose—one section or bullet point at a time, so you can keep your audience focused on the point you are currently making. If you don't use animation, and simply display the entire slide at once, the audience may read ahead, or become confused or distracted figuring out which point you are currently discussing. Therefore, use animation wisely and, at the same time, do not overload your slides with too much visual stimulation.

- *Build ideas with animation.* Your viewers will always read ahead of what you are saying. So if you want them to concentrate on the point you are currently discussing (such as on your agenda slide or on any other slide you want to go through slowly, explaining each point for some time), use animation to slow yourself down and to ensure enough time to cover each point.
- *Don't build too much.* On the other hand, remember that you do not need to . . .
    - Build
    - Every
    - Single
    - Point
    - On
    - Every
    - Single
    - Slide
- *Use a subtle animation effect.* PowerPoint offers a variety of animation effects—such as flying, dissolving, dropping down, swiveling, wiping, and even checkerboarding. Such excessive animation, with text flying in from every side and spinning, distracts your audience. Therefore, choose the Appear effect, in which your next point simply appears all at once, so your audience can focus on your content, not on dramatic and unnecessary movement on the screen.

3. Use "telegram language," not a script.

One way to avoid overloaded word-for-word script slides is to use what presentation expert Charlotte Rosen calls "telegram language"—that is, sentences or phrases minus most articles, auxiliary verbs, and prepositions.

Don't use text slides as scripts. Differentiate between your text slides and a script of your presentation or other written documents. Remember that text slides are . . .

- *For your audience:* Your slides are there to enhance audience understanding and retention, not for you to use as a crutch. So never use text slides as word-for-word scripts that duplicate what you are saying.
- *Slides, not document pages:* Your slides are not equivalent to a written document, such as a report. Therefore, never simply import an unedited Word document and use it as a slide. If you plan to simply read the text, you might as well save the audience time by emailing them your slides to read on their own; they can read three or four times faster than you can talk. Use complete sentences only when you are quoting someone word for word. In these cases, use quotation marks and provide the source of the quotation.
- *For emphasis only:* Your slides are for visual emphasis. If every single word you say is on the slides, your important ideas and concepts do not receive the emphasis they deserve.

Summarize the highlights only. Instead of word-for-word scripts, use short summaries of your key points. Then expand on those key points as you speak during your presentation. The following two examples show the agenda for the same presentation: the first in complete sentences, as a word-for-word script; the second edited down to key phrases only.

Ineffective: word-for-word script

INTRODUCTION

Over the past two decades, the waste management industry has undertaken planning as a response to growing markets and an increasingly competitive environment. Understanding historical environmental trends and how they are expected to change is critical to the development of successful strategies of Boford Industries. The purpose of this presentation is to

- Examine the waste management industry today and how it got there
- Assess future trends and their implications
- Discuss how other companies are reacting and changing in response to the external environment

Effective: key ideas only

Presentation Agenda
Boford Industries

- Examine historical trends
- Assess future trends
- Analyze competition

Use telegram language. Pare your wording. First, as you would in any writing, get rid of wordy and passive expressions. For example, write "about" instead of "in reference to," "recommend" rather than "make a recommendation," or "improve quality control" instead of "quality control should be improved."

Then for your slides, take the editing one step further by deleting most articles, auxiliary verbs, and prepositions.

Ineffective: does not use telegram language

XYZ Corporation has been downgraded by Moody's.
ABC has continued the push for globalization purchasing.

Effective: uses telegram language

Moody's downgrades XYZ.
ABC pushes for global purchasing.

Make sure your slides have stand-alone sense. At the same time that you reduce wordiness, make sure that the wording of your text slides makes "stand-alone sense"—that is, comprehensible to someone seeing it for the first time, to latecomers, or to someone reading hard copy of your slides later.

Ineffective bullet text: lacks stand-alone sense	*Effective bullet text: makes stand-alone sense*
Product	Unique business model
Market analysis	Large market with unmet needs
Competition	No direct competition
Operations	Institute a six-step process

4. Control the overall slide design.

Once you have edited the wording of your slide, check the slide's overall layout and appearance. Don't necessarily leave the design appearance the way it automatically appears after you type in the text.

Balance the overall appearance. Although your title and indentations should remain constant, as set in your Slide Master (as explained on page 50), check to make sure your text isn't crowded toward the top of the slide. Make your slide look balanced, rather than "top-right heavy," by changing the line spacing (explained on page 105).

Avoid "orphans." In those cases where the text of a bullet point continues (or "wraps") onto the next line, change the text to avoid having one word standing alone on a next line—what designers call an "orphan"—because one word alone looks lost on the slide.

Bad example with an orphan

Combining services leads to lower cost of
delivery

Improved version with no orphan

Combining services leads to
lower cost of delivery

Orphans are especially obvious in two-line slide titles. Insert a line break if necessary to keep logical phrases together.

Ineffective line break

New service offering will lead to value
added

Effective line break, with logical phrasing together

New service offering will
lead to value added

Avoid centering bullet texts. A common misunderstanding about visual design is that text should be centered. In reality, centering lines of text can make them harder to read. In most cases, use left justification for all text and all but one-line titles.

Centering text does not improve readability.
The lines may look balanced.
But left justification is still easier to read.
Centering long message titles looks odd, especially
when they wrap to the next line.

5. Use lettering, not "letterjunk."

In addition to getting rid of chartjunk (as discussed on pages 64–68) on text slides, be particularly aware of avoiding "letterjunk"—that is, any unnecessary use of fonts, case, and styles that does not add to your meaning.

Stick to your Slide Master. To review the guidelines we discussed in the Slide Master section (pages 42–44), you should use . . .

- *Sans serif font*, such as Arial or Verdana
- *Sentence case* (first word capitalized) for text; sentence or title case (initial letter of each word capitalized) for titles
- *Bold and italics* for titles and subtitles, never for extended text
- *Large enough letters:* titles 28 to 32 point, main text 18 to 24 point
- *Unobtrusive bullet characters*, such as filled circles, slightly smaller than your text and in the same color

Show relative importance. When choosing font styles or case, remember that some choices tend to look more emphatic than others.

ALL CAPS looks most emphatic.

Boldface or underlining looks somewhat emphatic.

Italics or regular text looks least emphatic.

Avoid letterjunk. As you compose your text slides, you may be tempted to use "letterjunk," styles or effects that detract from your slides' readability. To avoid letterjunk, do not use . . .

- *Styles for random words:* Random words within a phrase or sentence are not headings, so do not use font styles to set them off ***this way***. If you find yourself wanting to emphasize a word or phrase in the middle of your text, it is usually a sign that you need to move that word or phrase up front as a heading.
- *Too many styles and effects:* Do not use too many styles and effects all in the same lettering, like this . . .

BOLD PLUS ITALICS PLUS UNDERLINING

- *Unreadable effects:* Do not use unreadable font effects like this . . .

Shadow or embossing

- *Jarring font variations:* Stick to your Slide Master template.

Do not use *jarring* font variations.

- *Word Art:* Word Art is a feature that allows you to skew text in different directions and apply different effects to the letters. It is added by inserting a Word Art object on your slide. It is hard to read and looks amateurish.

Word Art distorts the fonts and usually looks amateurish

6. Check for correctness.

Do not undercut your credibility by having grammatical or spelling errors on your slides. These kinds of errors are even more noticeable and glaring on a large screen in front of a group of people than they are in a printed document. Therefore, be sure to double-check your text slides for the following issues.

Grammar and spelling errors: To check for spelling and grammatical errors, do not rely only on the built-in spell check feature of the software. Computers cannot check for (1) missing words or phrases; (2) all spelling errors (e.g., "you" for "your," or "on" for "of"); or (3) computer-generated errors, such as transferring only a part of a section or not deleting a phrase you changed. If possible, have someone who did not help create the slides read them "with a new pair of eyes" to check for such errors.

Parallelism: Make sure your bullet text at each hierarchical level is parallel.

- *Grammatical parallelism:* One kind of parallelism is grammatical—that is, the same grammatical construction for ideas of equal importance. For example, the first word in each bullet point could be an action verb, an *–ing* ending verb, a pronoun, or whatever—but it must be consistent with the first words in the other bullet points in that particular series. Starting each bullet with an action verb (such as "Modify," "Research," "Plan," or "Execute") makes your text more action-oriented and has a greater impact on the audience.
- *Conceptual parallelism:* Bullets must not only be grammatically parallel, but also conceptually parallel—that is, each heading should be the same kind of item.

Ineffective headings: not conceptually parallel, although grammatically parallel

Cost-Effective Optimization

- What are the two options?
- What are the problems with Testing?
- What is Finite Element Analysis (FEA)?
- What are the benefits of FEA?

Effective headings: conceptually parallel

Cost-Effective Optimization

- Option 1: Testing
- Option 2: FEA

Correct use of bullets: Use bullet points thoughtfully, not randomly. As we mentioned in Chapter 7, visuals expert Edward Tufte points out (in his diatribe against "death by bullet list") that the relationship among the three points in the following bullet list is unclear:

Bullet list: relationship among points unclear

- Increase market share
- Increase profits
- Increase number of new products

In contrast, the following concept diagrams show three possible relationships among the same three points:

Concept diagrams: relationships are clear

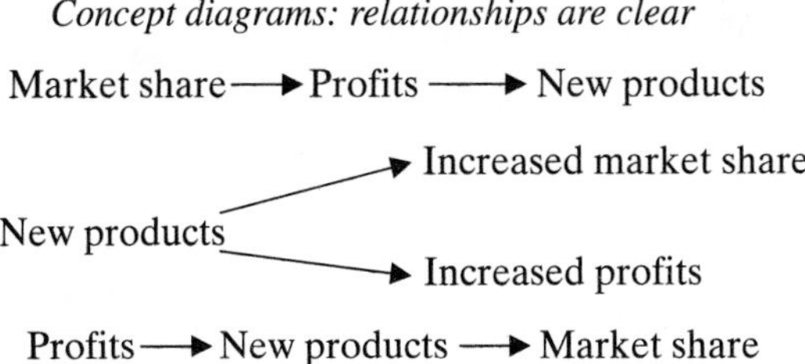

Make it clear if your bullet list is (1) a sequence (first to last), (2) priority (most to least, or vice versa), or (3) membership in a set. For any other relationships among your points, use a concept diagram (as explained on pages 80–85).

- *When you have at least two items:* Never use a single bullet point. Use bullets only if you have at least two items listed in any given set.
- *Instead of numbers:* Use bullets instead of numbers for the items on your list unless you want to (1) imply relative importance, (2) imply a time sequence, or (3) refer to items by number.

II. HOW TO DO IT

Note: If you do not understand any of the following instructions or terms, please see the Glossaries, pages 167–183.

This section tells you how to compose text slides, change text format, and import text from Word.

1. To compose text slides

To add the slide title:

- Click in the title box ❶ → Type the title.

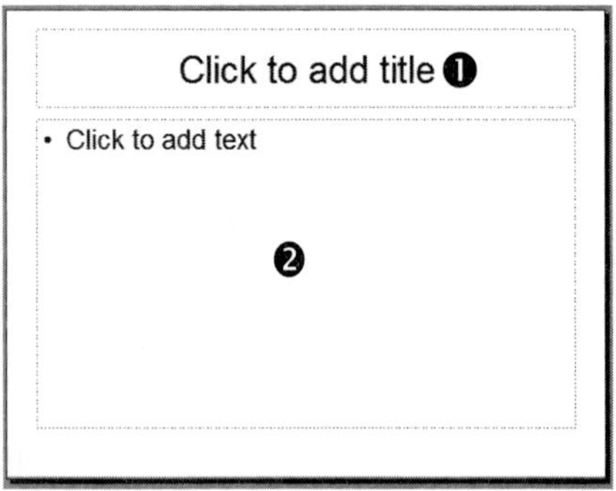

To add main text points:

- Click in the body text box ❷ → Type the text.
- *To start a new bullet point*: Press the Enter key.
- *To break a line before the line automatically wraps*: Hold the Shift key down and press the Enter key.
- *To move to a lower level of bullet point*: Press the Tab key at the start of the bullet point.
- *To return to the previous level of bullet point*: Hold the Shift key down and press the Tab key at the start of the bullet point.

To edit existing text:

- Click at the spot in the text → Use the Delete key, Backspace key, or type more text.

To copy text:

- Highlight the text → Copy the text → Position the cursor where the text should be copied to (maybe on a different slide) → Paste the text.

To move text:

- Highlight the text → Cut the text → Position the cursor where the text should be moved to (maybe on a different slide) → Paste the text.

2. To change text format

When you set up your Slide Master, you chose your text font, size, and color to be consistent throughout your entire presentation (as explained on page 46). In general, you should not deviate from your Slide Master, because changing the appearance of text on different slides makes your presentation look incoherent and may distract or confuse your audience.

However, if for some reason you want to deviate from your Slide Master, you can modify your text appearance by (1) highlighting the text you want to change, and (2) using the tools on the Formatting toolbar usually found at the top of the screen (if it is not there, you can display it by clicking View → Toolbars → Formatting).

Formatting Toolbar

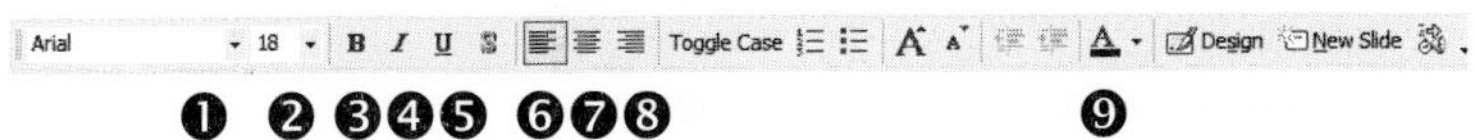

To change the font face: Click the font face drop-down menu ❶ → Select a font face.

To change the font size: Click the font size drop-down menu ❷ → Select a font size.

To change the font style: Click the bold ❸, italic ❹, or underline ❺ toolbar buttons.

To change the text alignment: Click the left ❻, center ❼, or right ❽ alignment toolbar buttons.

To change the font color: Click the font color toolbar drop-down menu ❾ → Select a new color.

To change line spacing:

- Click Format → Line Spacing.
- Select the spacing by Lines ❶ (e.g., double-space, single-space, etc.) → Click Preview ❷ to see what it will look like → Click OK ❸ .

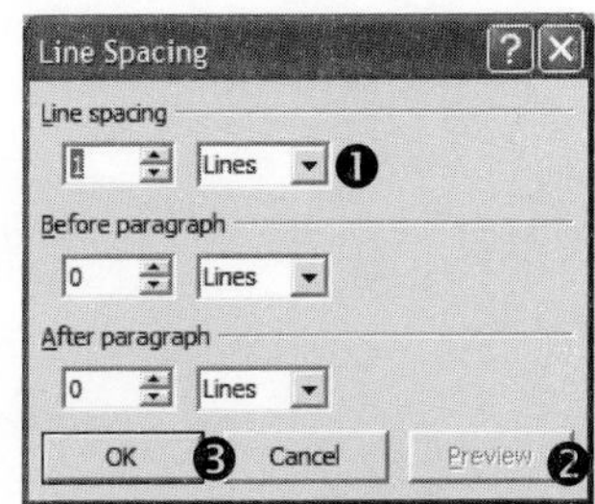

To change slide layout:

- Click Format → Slide Layout.
- Click the layout you want (title only, single column, double column, etc.) ❶.

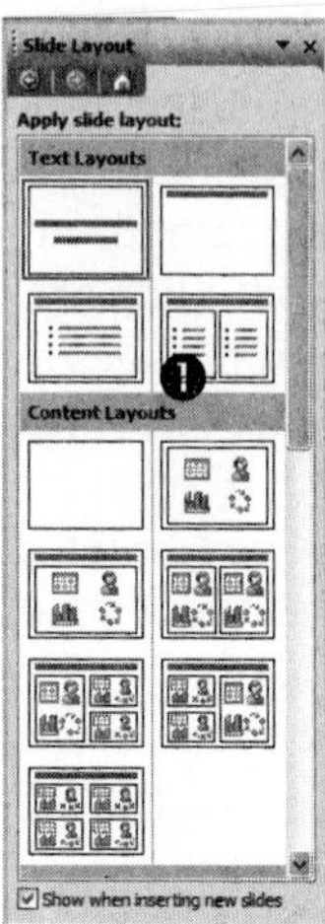

To animate the text to build bullet by bullet:

- Click Slide Show → Custom Animation.
- Click on the body text box
  → Click Add Effect ❶
  → Click Entrance ❷
  Click Appear ❸.

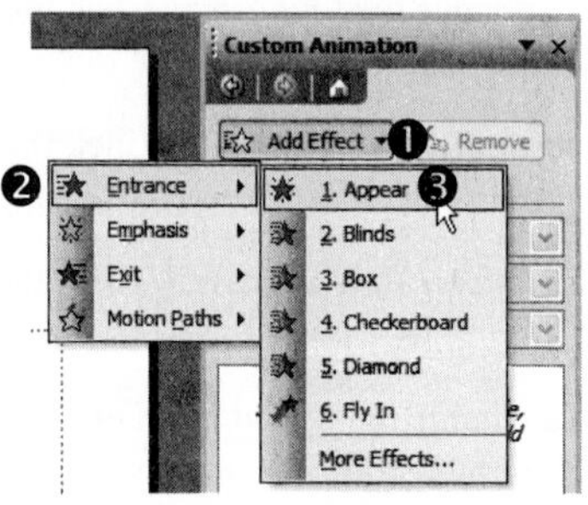

To animate the text to build subpoints:

- Click on text element animation in list ❶ → Click the drop-down arrow ❷ → Click Effect Options ❸.

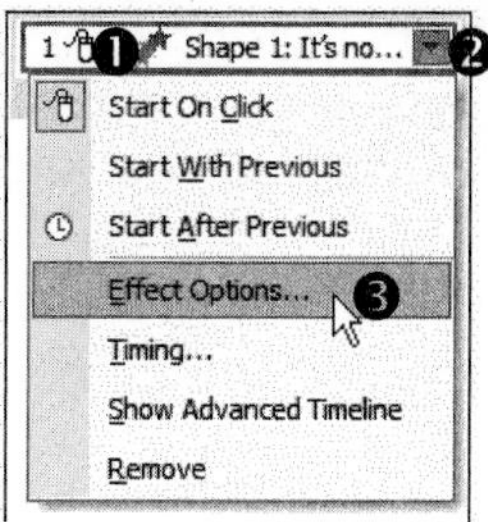

- Click Text Animation ❶ → Click Group text drop-down arrow ❷ → Select By 2nd or By 3rd level paragraphs ❸ to build each subgroup in bulleted text → Click OK ❹.

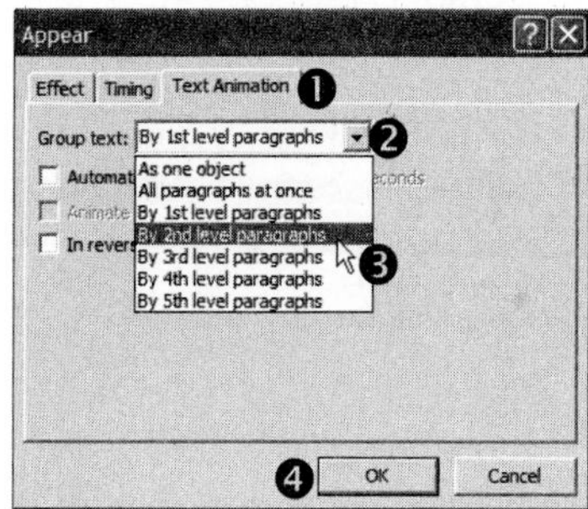

3. To import text from Word

If you have written your text slides in Word, you can import that content into your slides. Each new page will become a separate slide; the hierarchical levels of the bullet points in Word will automatically transfer onto your slides.

To create a text slide in Word:

- Create a new Word document.
- From the Formatting task pane (accessed by clicking Format → Styles and Formatting), set the Heading 1, 2, and 3 styles ❶ according to the guidelines on pages 42–44.
- Create your slides: (1) title on first line, (2) text for bullet points each on a separate line.
- Format the text: (1) titles using the Heading 1 style, (2) first-level bullet points using the Heading 2 style, (3) second-level bullet points using the Heading 3 style.
- Save the document and close it. (PowerPoint will not import the file if it is still open in Word.)

Example: Word document

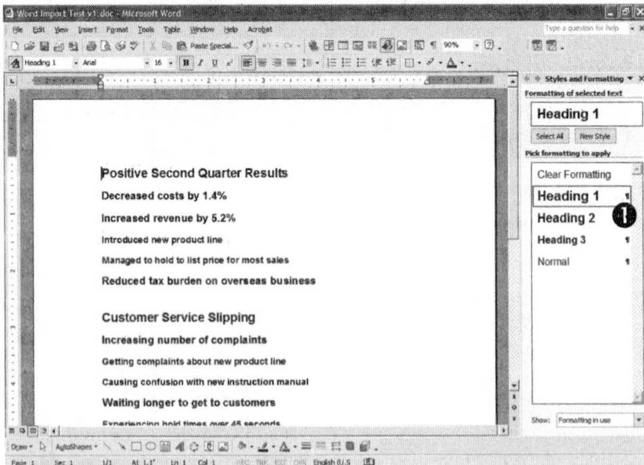

To import the Word document into PowerPoint: When you import documents from Word, they will be converted into slides based on the Heading styles you chose in Word.

- Open a new PowerPoint file.
- Click Insert → Slides From Outline.
- Select the Word file that you previously saved from the file list shown → Click Insert.

Example: imported slide

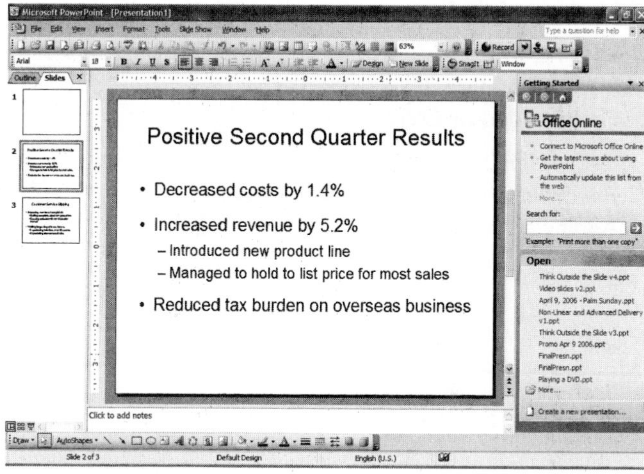

CHAPTER OUTLINE

I. USING PHOTOGRAPHS
   1. Selecting and inserting photos
   2. Modifying photos

II. USING CLIP ART
   1. Choosing effective Clip Art
   2. Finding Clip Art
   3. Modifying Clip Art

III. USING VIDEO
   1. Inserting and modifying video
   2. Playing video or DVD

IV. USING AUDIO
   1. Recording, selecting, and storing audio
   2. Adding audio
   3. Playing the audio

CHAPTER 9

Other Slide Enhancements

PowerPoint offers many options for enhancing your slides beyond the basic charts, diagrams, and text slides. These enhancements include photographs, Clip Art, video, and audio. To decide when each option might be appropriate, keep in mind the following advantages and potential problems.

Advantages: These options can enhance your presentation because they can . . .

- Add a visual aspect to the text that is on the slide
- Provide visual variety to keep the audience's attention
- Make a point come alive in the audience's mind, thereby increasing their likelihood of remembering your ideas

Potential problems: Although these options can be beneficial, they can also lead to problems if they send . . .

- *The wrong message:* If "a picture is worth a thousand words," the wrong picture will say the wrong thousand words. Be sure that the picture will increase the impact of your message, not detract from it.
- *An inconsistent message:* Don't leave your audience wondering what your point really is by using a slide option that is inconsistent with the message you are trying to get across with the particular slide. Select each option extremely carefully: do not just casually toss in a photo or some Clip Art because it is so easy and inviting to do so.
- *A confusing message:* Finally, remember that too many of these options, with no accompanying text, can confuse your audience because they have no way to put the graphics into context.

I. USING PHOTOGRAPHS

The ability to use photographs is a wonderful tool in PowerPoint. Use this tool wisely—to enhance your message, not distract your audience. With that advice in mind, use the following techniques to select, insert, and modify photos.

1. Selecting and inserting photos

Photographs are available from a wide variety of sources. When selecting them, in addition to the caveats listed on the previous page, remember to . . .

- Choose photos that are not widely used.
- Make sure that the photograph's colors contrast well with your slide background so that it can be seen.

Choose a source. The following table outlines five sources of photos for your presentation: from PowerPoint, your own digital pictures, your own scanned-in pictures, online photo libraries, and purchased photo collections. It is illegal to copy photos from the Internet (including newspaper, magazine, and company websites). Photos on websites are copyrighted: you do not have permission to use them, except in the rare event that the web page specifically states you can do so.

SOURCES OF PHOTOS		
Available from ...	**Advantages**	**Disadvantages**
Microsoft (in PowerPoint or on their Office Online Clip Art and Media website)	• Easy to access • No cost • Good search feature	• May be small in size • Low resolution • Commonly used
Your digital photos	• Always unique • Exactly what you want • High resolution • Easy to do • Unlimited usage	• Requires a digital camera and some training • Can't always take a photo when you need it
Scanned-in printed photos	• Allows use of historical photos • High resolution • Widely available	• Need access to a scanner • May violate copyright if you don't own the photo • May be hard to find the right photo when needed
Online photo libraries (e.g. www.istockphoto.com)	• Many photos from which to choose • Available in different sizes	• Can be costly • May not be easy to search • May have limits on use of photos
Purchased photo collections on CD or DVD (e.g., Fotosearch)	• Many photos in each category • Available in different sizes	• Can be expensive if you buy many collections • Collections are usually limited to one theme • May have limits on use of photos

Save the photos on your computer. Before you can insert the photo onto a slide, you need to save it on your computer. If the source is . . .

- *Your digital camera:* Use the software that came with the camera to transfer the photo from the camera into a computer file.
- *A scanned photo:* Use the scanner and the software that came with it to scan the photo and save the photo file to your computer.
- *An online image bank:* Save the photo file to your computer as you download it from the website.
- *A purchased photo collection:* Copy the photo file to your computer using the software or instructions that came with the collection disc.

"Resize and resample" high-resolution photos. The problem with high-resolution photos is that they are stored as large files, which can cause your PowerPoint presentation file to become very large. These large files will (1) be hard to work with and to send to others, and (2) cause the slide to load slowly, usually with a noticeable delay and an uncomfortable pause in the presentation. Fortunately, you can use a technique called "resize and resample" to avoid having them take up enormous amounts of storage space.

To do so, use photo software (such as Adobe Photoshop) or a utility called IrfanView (available at www.irfanview.com). This process will result in a high-quality image with a much smaller file size and quicker operation. In either photo software or IrfanView, resize and resample the photo by setting the following two parameters:

- *Choose number of pixels needed:* (1) If you want the photo to fill the entire slide, then choose a resolution of 1024 pixels wide by 768 pixels high, which is standard XGA resolution. (2) If you are using a small photo on the slide, then a resolution of 150 pixels wide will be sufficient.
- *Keep a constant height/width ratio.* Regardless of what size you select, when you resize and resample, always make sure that you set the option to keep the height/width ratio (also known as the aspect ratio) constant (as explained on page 175). By doing so, you keep the ratio of width to height in the photo constant so that the photo does not look stretched or squashed in one direction.
- *Use a new name:* Use a new name when you save the resized and resampled photo so that your original file does not get overwritten (in case you need to use the higher-resolution photo to print at a later time).

Insert the photo on a slide.

- Click Insert → Picture → From File.
- Select the desired photo file → Click OK.

2. Modifying photos

Once you have inserted the photos into your slides, you can modify them to make them even more effective. Here are some of the most common changes.

To move: Position the photo where you want it to be on the slide. If the photo takes up the whole slide, make sure it is indeed covering the entire slide and not hanging off one side. If it is the main focus of the slide, center it. If it is not the main focus, position it close to a lower corner of the slide so that it does not draw attention away from the main focus of the slide.

- Click on the photo.
- Drag it to the correct place on the slide.
- Hold the Ctrl key down and use the arrow keys to move the photo a small amount (one pixel) at a time.

To resize: Think about how big you want the photo to be. Sometimes it will take up the entire slide; if not, make sure it does not dominate the slide and detract from the text.

- Click on the photo.
- Click on a corner handle ❶ and drag the handle to produce the correct size.
- Hold the Shift key down while dragging to maintain the height/width ratio.

For all of the following modifications, you will be working from the Picture Toolbar. To get to that toolbar . . .

- Click on the photo and the Picture Toolbar should appear.
- If the Picture Toolbar does not appear, click View → Toolbars → Picture.

Picture Toolbar

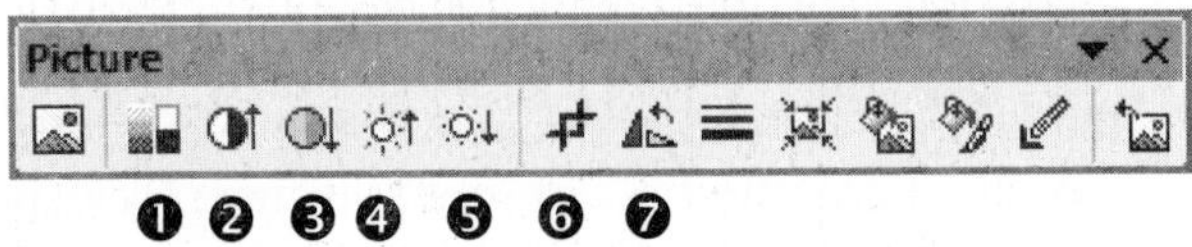

To adjust color for effects: You can also adjust the color to achieve certain effects. For example, you might use (1) grayscale to make the photo look as if it were taken with black and white film, (2) black and white to make it look like a modern art rendering of the photo, or (3) "washout" to decrease the brightness or prominence of the photo.

- Click on the color effects toolbar button ❶ in the Picture Toolbar.
- Select one of the options.

To adjust brightness or contrast: The brightness and contrast of photos have a large impact on how they look on screen. Brightness will affect the amount of black or white added to the colors and contrast affects the intensity of the colors in the photo. Many times a photo will look darker when projected than it did on your computer monitor. Therefore, either (1) check your photos on the large screen before the presentation, or (2) be prepared to test and adjust them when you set up for your presentation.

- Click on the increase ❷ or decrease ❸ contrast toolbar buttons in the Picture Toolbar and you will see the photo change.
- Click on the increase ❹ or decrease ❺ brightness toolbar buttons in the Picture Toolbar and you will see the photo change.

To crop: Decide what the most important part of the photo is and "crop out" (that is, eliminate) the rest of the photo.

- Click on the cropping button in the Picture Toolbar ❻.
- Drag one of the cropping handles (the black bars at any corner or side of the photo) to crop the photo from that edge.
- Click on the cropping button in the Picture Toolbar again to complete the cropping.

To rotate: You might also want to rotate the photo vertically or horizontally.

- Click on the rotate icon in the Picture Toolbar ❼.
- The photo will rotate 90 degrees each time you click the button.

II. USING CLIP ART

Many presenters find Clip Art (that is, ready-made illustrations or artwork) an easy way to spice up their slides. The problem with Clip Art, however, is that it can be overused, clichéd, or just plain silly, or it can be a visual intrusion, clutter, or chartjunk (that is, any design element that does not add to your meaning, as explained on pages 64–68).

1. Choosing effective Clip Art

Before you choose to use Clip Art, make sure it is . . .

Meaningful: Just because it's easy to find and insert Clip Art doesn't mean you should use it. Use Clip Art only when it adds to your message; don't use it if it actually detracts from your message because your audience is concentrating on it instead of your message.

Not intrusive or clichéd: Make sure the image looks current and fresh, not hackneyed (for example, the head-scratching "screen bean" characters).

In a visible color: Be careful about the colors of the Clip Art image. It must have strong enough contrast with your slide background color to be seen well. If you usually use a dark background for your presentation slides, try to pick bright-colored Clip Art. In general, avoid black Clip Art unless you are using a light-colored background because it is hard to see black on top of most dark colors.

Not animated: The most intrusive and distracting examples of Clip Art are animated GIFs (Graphics Interchange Format). These animations show cartoon-like movement, which distract your audience both because of their constant movement and because they are overused as annoying advertisements on the web.

2. Finding Clip Art

There are two main sources for Clip Art: Power Point based and web based.

To search in PowerPoint: PowerPoint contains a large number of Clip Art images from which to choose. However, so many people use these standard images that they do not stand out anymore. Instead, look for new ones in Clip Art software packages that you can buy or that are available for free on the Internet.

- *To open the Insert Clip Art task pane:*
  —Click Insert → Picture → Clip Art.
- *To search for an appropriate Clip Art image:*
  —Enter one search term in the Search Text box ❶ (e.g., "truck" in the example at right).
  —Click the "Results should be" drop–down arrow ❷ → Uncheck boxes for Photographs, Movies, and Sounds ❸ .
  —Click Go ❹ .

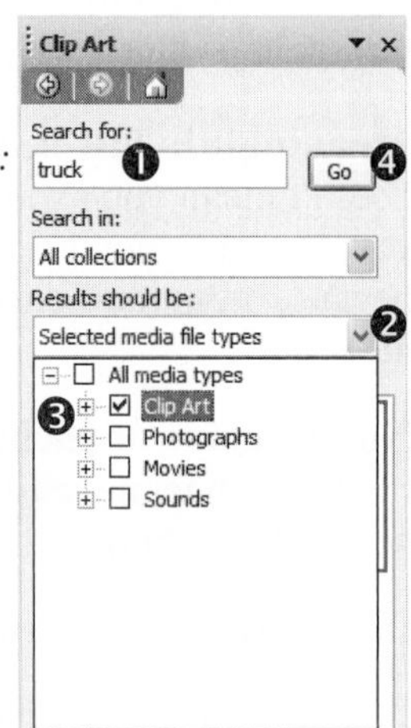

- *To insert Clip Art:*
  —The search will display Clip Art that matches your search criteria. Scroll through the images to find one you want to use.
  —Position the cursor over the image thumbnail in the task pane ❶ → Click arrow on right side of image ❷ → Click Insert ❸ on the submenu that appears.

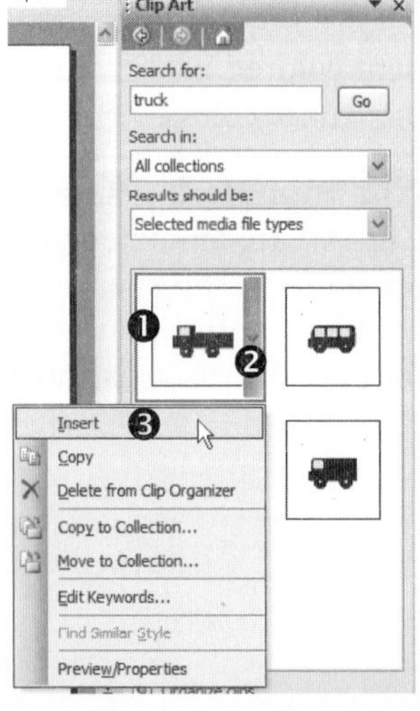

To search in web-based collections: One of the best sources we have found is the Microsoft Office Online Clip Art and Media website at http://office.microsoft.com/clipart/default.aspx. This website is automatically loaded when you ask PowerPoint's Clip Art function to find an image on the web. When you enter a search term, it displays those Clip Art images that match the keyword you entered. This function allows you to select images that most others are not using because the database contains more than 140,000 multimedia items with new ones added frequently.

- Click the Clip art on Office Online link at the bottom of the Insert Clip Art task pane ❶ to go to the Microsoft Office Clip Art and Media web page.

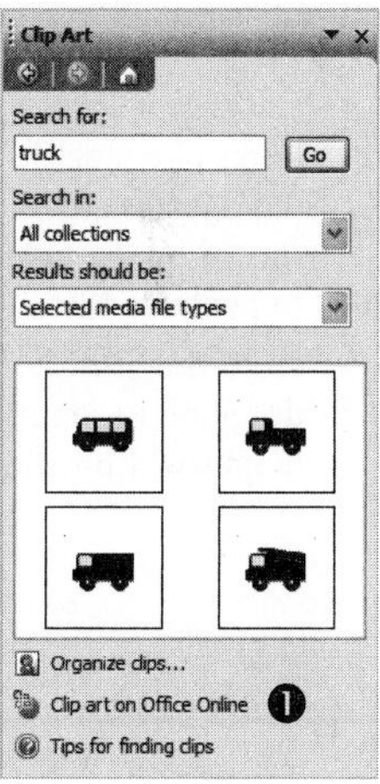

- Enter your search term ❶ and select what type of media you want to search for ❷.

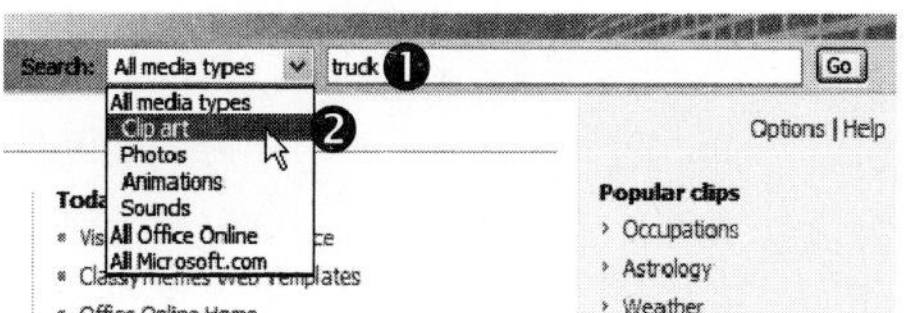

- Position your cursor over the desired image in the search results and click on the drop-down arrow that appears on the right side of the image → Click Copy.
- Return to your slide and Paste the image.

3. Modifying Clip Art

Once the Clip Art is on your slide, you can move it, resize it, or change its colors.

To move Clip Art on the slide:

- Click on the Clip Art.
- Drag it to the correct place.

To resize Clip Art:

- Click on the Clip Art.
- Click on a corner handle (which looks like a circle) ❶ and drag the handle in either direction (as shown by the slanted arrow at right) to produce the correct size.
- Hold the Shift key down while dragging to maintain the height/width ratio.

To change Clip Art colors:

- Right-click on the Clip Art image → Click Format Picture in the sub-menu that appears.
- Click on the Picture tab ❶ → Click the Recolor button ❷ to display the Recolor Picture dialog box.

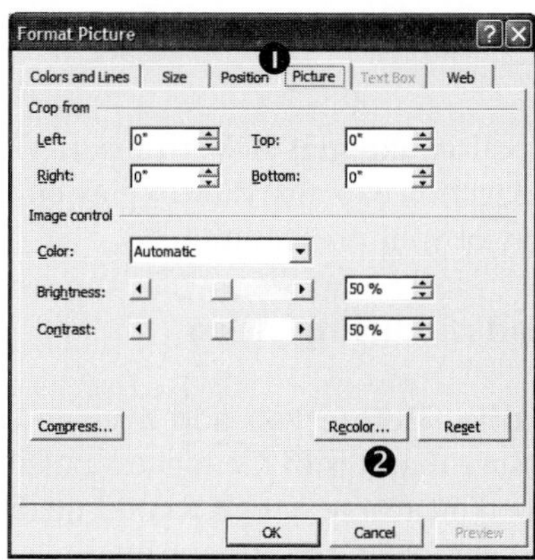

- Select new colors to replace the original colors ❶.
- Click OK.

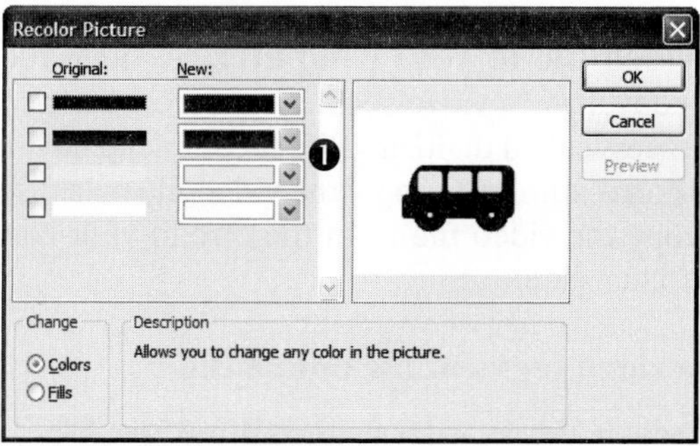

III. USING VIDEO

Like all the other slide options, video should be used for one purpose only: to increase the impact of the message. You can use video in either of two ways in your presentation:

- Insert a video file on your computer into a PowerPoint slide and play it in PowerPoint.
- Play a DVD disc on your computer (if it supports DVDs) or on a DVD player.

The following section explains how to insert video into PowerPoint; the second section explains how to play either a video file or a DVD on the day of your presentation.

1. Inserting and modifying video

Check the quality. Before you add a video segment to your presentation, be sure that it is of the highest possible quality. When a video is magnified on a large screen, a good-quality video segment will remain crisp and clear, but a poor-quality segment will look even blurrier and fuzzier than it did on your computer monitor.

Therefore, when you watch the video segment on your TV or monitor screen, look closely for areas that are fuzzy, distorted, or unclear. Minor distractions on a small screen will appear as major distractions on a large screen.

Save the video file to your computer. A video file is usually created by converting a video segment to a computer readable file format, a process called digitizing. We recommend having this done by a professional, who will supply the video file on a disc for you to use. Then copy the video file from the disc to your computer and insert it onto the slide.

To insert a video segment file onto a slide:

- Click Insert → Movies and Sounds → Movie from File.
- Select the file containing the video segment → Click OK.
- When the software asks you when you want the video segment to play, click Automatically ❶ (shown on the facing page) if you want the video segment to play as soon as the slide is displayed. Click When Clicked ❷ if you want to control when the video segment is played on the slide.

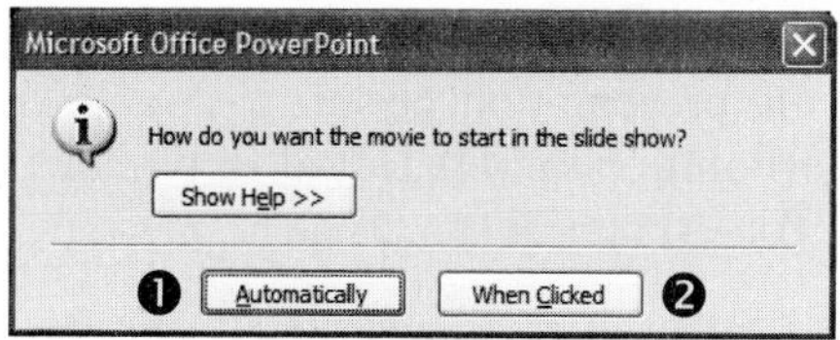

To resize the video segment to make it larger and easier to see:

- Click on the video segment on the slide.
- Click and drag one of the corner handles of the video segment box ❶ to make it larger.

To set when the video segment starts playing (if you did not select to have it automatically play when you inserted it):

- Click Slide Show → Custom Animation.
- Right-click the video segment listed in the list of animation elements ❶ → Click Effect Options ❷.

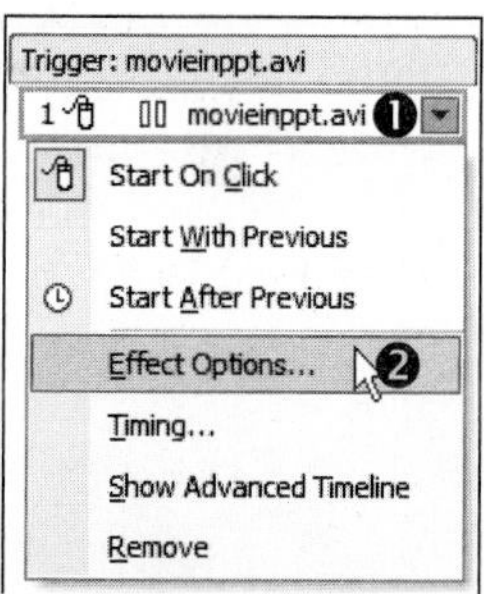

- Click the Timing tab ❶ → Select Animate as part of click sequence (the sequence in which items appear on the slide) ❷ → Click OK.

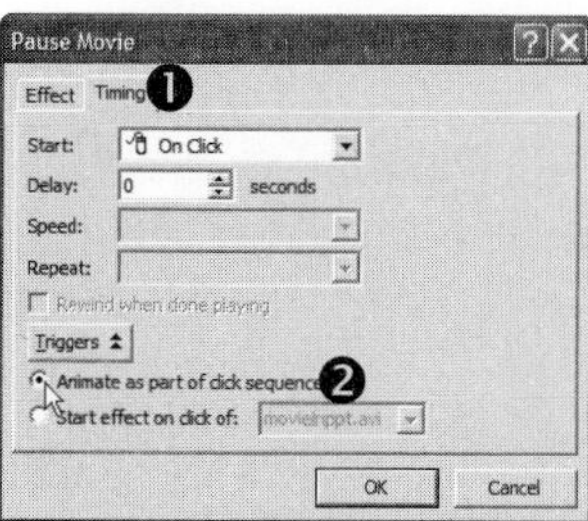

2. Playing video or DVD

On the day of your presentation, be sure to double-check the video quality in PowerPoint or the DVD and to practice until you can play it easily in PowerPoint or the DVD.

Test it. Test both the video (how it looks) and the audio (how it sounds).

- *Test the video:* Watch the video from the back of the meeting room to see whether it is clearly visible from the last row of chairs. (1) *If it is too small,* you can enlarge it by moving the projector farther away from the screen. (2) *If the screen is already filled* and the video segment is still too small, you might choose not to use the video at all, because those who can't see it may be annoyed. To hide the slide that contains the video segment, Click on the slide → Click Slide Show → Hide Slide.
- *Test the audio:* Make sure that the audio outputs of the computer or the DVD player are connected. Test the volume to make sure everyone will be able to hear it clearly.

Play the video segment from PowerPoint: When the video segment is part of a PowerPoint slide, it will start either automatically when the slide is shown or as part of the click sequence, depending on which option you chose when you created the slide.

Play the DVD: If you have a DVD disc, you have two options for showing it: (1) on DVD-playing software in your computer, or (2) on a regular DVD player that is connected to the data projector.

- *Option 1: On your computer:* Before your presentation, start the DVD-playing software and load the video segment so that it is ready to play.

  When you want to play the video: (1) Press Alt+Tab to switch from your presentation to the DVD-playing software. (You may have to press Alt+Tab more than once if you have other programs open.) (2) Play the video segment using the appropriate method for your DVD playing software (usually by pressing a Play button to start the DVD-playing). (3) When the video segment is finished, stop the DVD (usually by pressing a Stop button) and press Alt+Tab to return to your presentation. (Again, you may have to press Alt+Tab more than once if you have other programs open.)

- *Option 2: On a DVD player:* Before the presentation, connect the DVD player to the projector, using the projector input for a video source (which is a different input from the one connected to the computer). The input source button on the projector allows you to switch the input back and forth between the computer and the video input. Make sure to practice the transition between the two input sources so you can do it seamlessly during the presentation.

  When you want to play the video: (1) Use the input source button on the projector to switch the display input on the projector from your computer to the video equipment. (2) Press the Play button on the DVD player to start the video segment. (3) When the video segment is completed, press the Stop button on the DVD player and use the input source button on the projector to switch the display input on the projector back to the computer input.

IV. USING AUDIO

Adding audio to your presentation can increase the impact of your message. For example, you can play music or other sound effects to emphasize a point you are making, or you can play an audio of a person saying his or her own quotation, instead of just showing it written on the screen. However, like all other options discussed in this chapter, audio should be used for one purpose only: to increase the impact of the message.

Keep in mind, however, that when it is amplified through a sound system, the quality of an audio segment is magnified. Therefore, (1) a poor-quality audio segment sounds even worse and more distorted when it is amplified, and (2) even a good-quality audio segment can become distorted if it is played too loudly.

1. Recording, selecting, and storing audio

Although you want to have the highest quality sound possible, the higher the sound quality, the larger the file size will be on both your recording device and your computer. So if your storage space is limited or you will be distributing the file via email or CD, you may need to ask an audio professional to adjust the quality down in order to create a smaller file.

Recording audio files:

- *Recording yourself:* If you are recording the audio segment yourself, set the parameters in the recording software to give you the best quality possible. Check your recording software documentation for instructions on setting the various parameters. We recommend (1) most importantly, a "sample rate" as high as possible (by way of comparison, a CD has a sample rate of 44,100 hertz; a telephone has a rate of only 8,000 hertz); (2) a "bit rate" of at least 128; and (3) stereo rather than mono.
- *Recording in a studio:* If you are having the audio segment recorded in a studio, ask the studio staff to record at a quality level equivalent to a commercial CD.

Selecting audio files: If you are using a pre-recorded audio segment, listen carefully to the audio with headphones to see whether it has any distortion or annoying sounds in it.

Storing audio files: Once you have the audio file recorded or selected, you have two options for storing it.

- *Store on your computer:* If you are going to store audio files on your computer, you will need to copy the file from your source, usually a disc or an email sent from the recording studio, to your computer.
- *Store on audio CD:* You can also choose to store your audio file in audio CD format, in which case you have the choice to play the audio from a CD player or your computer.

2. Adding audio

Use these instructions if the audio is stored on your computer.

To insert an audio file:

- Click Insert → Movies and Sounds → Sound from File.
- Select the audio file on your computer → Click OK.
- Click Automatically ❶ if you want the audio file to play as soon as the slide is displayed. Click When Clicked ❷ if you want to control when the audio file is played on the slide.

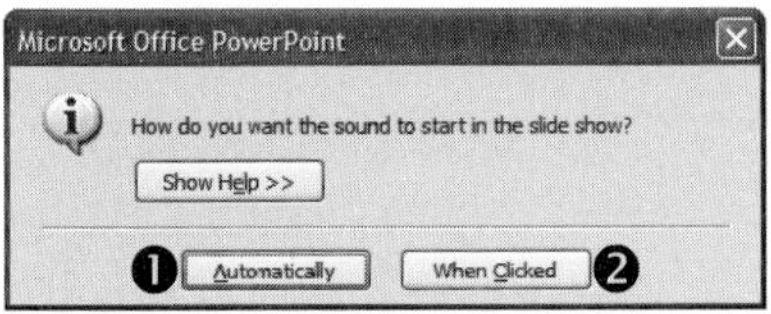

To hide the audio icon:

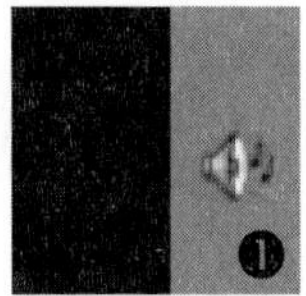

- Drag the speaker icon that represents the audio clip off the slide so it is not seen when the slide is projected ❶.

- To set when the audio file starts playing (if you did not set it to play automatically when you inserted the audio file) (1) Click Slide Show → Custom Animation. (2) Right-click the audio clip listed ❶ → Click Effect Options ❷.

- Click Timing ❶ → Select Animate as part of click sequence ❷.
- Click OK.

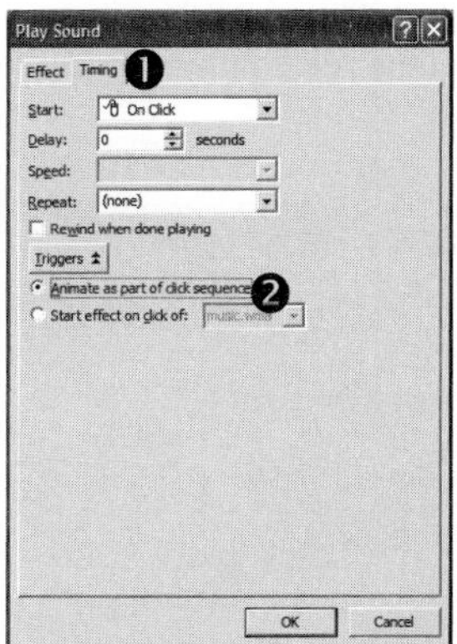

To set audio play options:

- Click Slide Show → Custom Animation.
- Right-click the audio clip listed ❶ → Click Effect Options ❷.

- Click Effect ❶.
- If you want the audio clip to continue playing after this slide, set the stop playing setting ❷ to the number of slides you want to display before the audio clip stops.
- Click the Sound Volume speaker icon ❸ and use the slider ❹ to set the playback volume.

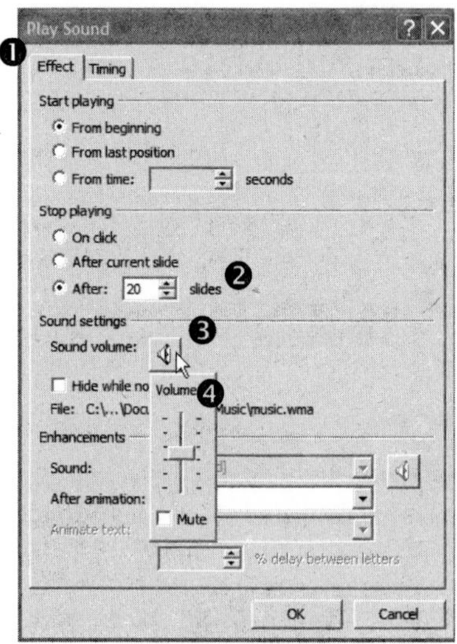

- Click Timing ❶.
- Use the Repeat setting ❷ if you want the audio file to play more than once.
- Click OK.

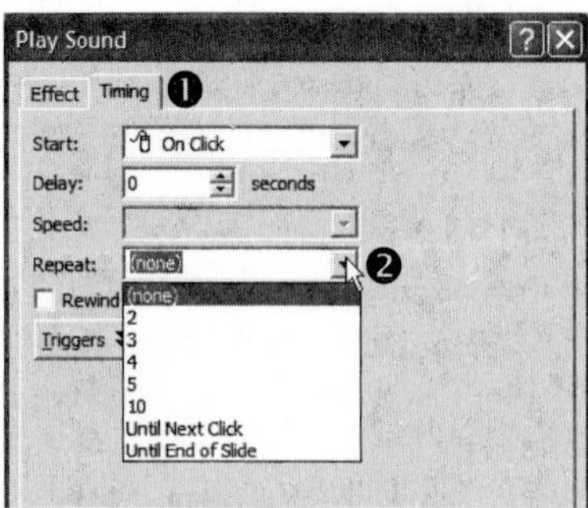

3. Playing the audio

You have four options for playing the audio during your presentation. Whichever method you choose, however, test the audio quality at a volume amplified to the level you will use for the actual presentation, not just through headphones or the speakers of your computer. If you are using option 3 or 4 (below), practice the transition between your presentation and playing the audio CD until you can perform it smoothly.

Option 1: Play automatically when slide is displayed: If you set it to play automatically, the audio file will start playing as soon as the slide is displayed; you do not have to do anything to make it play.

Option 2: Play as part of a click sequence: If you selected to play the audio file as part of a click sequence (part of the sequence of animation for this slide), click the down arrow or other advance method to start the audio file playing. If you are using a presentation remote you can press the advance key to start the audio file playing.

Option 3: Play an audio CD on your computer media player: Before the presentation, start the media player program (such as Windows Media Player or Real Audio Player) on your computer and load the CD so that it is ready to play. When you want to play the audio CD during your presentation . . .

- Press Alt+Tab to switch from the PowerPoint presentation to the media player. (You may have to press Alt+Tab more than once if you have other applications open.)
- Press the Play button in the media player program to start playing the CD. (Some media players take a long time to start playing, which may cause a long pause in the presentation.)
- Once the CD has finished playing, press the Stop button in the media player program.
- Press Alt+Tab to return to the PowerPoint presentation. (Again, you may have to press Alt+Tab more than once if you have other applications open.)

Option 4: Play an audio CD on a CD player: Before the presentation, connect the CD player to the sound system or speakers. Load the CD in the CD player and set it to the spot you want to play during the presentation. When you want the audio to play, use the Play button on the CD player. Once the CD is played, press the Stop button on the CD player.

PART IV

Presentation Delivery

CHAPTER OUTLINE

I. NONVERBAL SKILLS
   1. Body language
   2. Vocal qualities
   3. Space and objects
   4. Practice and arrangements

II. RELAXATION TECHNIQUES
   1. Physical relaxation
   2. Mental relaxation
   3. Last-minute relaxation

CHAPTER 10

Nonverbal Delivery

After all the work you've done on your slides, it's sometimes hard to remember that your words and your visuals make up only a portion of what you communicate. In fact, experts estimate that 65 to 90 percent of what you communicate is nonverbal. This chapter covers those nonverbal messages you send—the way you appear and sound to others. Nonverbal delivery skills include body language, vocal qualities, and the use of space and objects around you. In addition, the chapter covers various methods for combating stage fright: physical, mental, and last-minute relaxation techniques.

I. NONVERBAL SKILLS

Nonverbal delivery skills include body language, vocal qualities, and space and objects around you. After we analyze each of these skills, we offer some practice techniques to improve your nonverbal delivery.

1. Body language

Keep in mind these five elements of body language.

Posture: Effective speakers exhibit poise through their posture.

- Stand in a relaxed, professional manner—comfortably upright, squarely facing your audience, with your weight balanced and distributed evenly. Your feet should be aligned under your shoulders, neither too close nor too far apart.
- Watch out for (1) rocking, swaying, or bouncing; (2) leaning, slouching, or the "hip sit"; (3) "frozen" poses such as the stiff "Attention!" or the wide-legged "cowpoke straddle" stances.

Body movement: Body movement varies by personality and room size.

- Move naturally. You don't have to stand stock still or plan every move. Examples of effective body movement include leaning forward to emphasize a point or moving to the other side of the screen for part of your presentation.
- Avoid random, nervous, quick, or constant movements.

Hand and arm gestures: Effective speakers use their hands the same way they would conversationally.

- Let your hands do whatever they would be doing if you were speaking to one person instead of a group. Be yourself: some people use expansive gestures; others are more reserved. For example, use them to move as you would in a conversation, to be still for a while, to emphasize a point, to describe an object, or to point to a particular spot on the screen.
- Avoid putting your hands in any one position and leaving them there without change—such as the "fig leaf" (hands clasped in front), the "parade rest" (hands clasped in back), the "gunshot wound" (hand clutching opposite arm), or the "podium clutch." Avoid nervous-looking gestures, such as ear-tugging or arm-scratching. Finally, avoid "authority killers" like flipping your hair or waving your arms randomly.

Facial expression: Your facial expression should also look natural as it would in conversation.

- Keep your face relaxed to look interested and animated. Vary your expression according to the subject and the occasion.
- Avoid a stony, deadpan expression; also, avoid inappropriate facial expression, such as smiling when you are talking about something sad or negative.

Eye contact: Eye contact is a crucial nonverbal skill. It makes possible what communication expert Lynn Russell calls the "listener/speaker connection": the audience feels connected with you and you feel connected with them and can read their reactions.

- *Do look* throughout the entire room, establishing momentary (that is, about two-second) contact with individuals in your audience. You might try, for starters, looking at the friendly faces; their nodding and smiling will encourage you. Eventually, however, you should look at everyone—especially the key decision makers in the group. You don't need to keep 100 percent eye contact; you may need to look away briefly to think. If, after your presentation, you can remember what the people in your audience looked like, you had good eye contact.
- *Avoid looking* constantly at a manuscript or note cards, at the slides or screen, at the middle of the back of the room, at the ceiling, or at the floor. Don't show a preference for looking at one side of the room or the other. Finally, avoid fake eye contact—such as the rapid around-the-room "eye dart," or the slow back-and-forth "lighthouse scan."

2. Vocal qualities

Many people underestimate the importance of the voice in establishing credibility. See page 143 for vocal relaxation exercises.

Inflection and volume: The term "inflection" refers to variation in your pitch, which creates an expressive, nonmonotonous sound; "volume" refers to how loudly you speak.

- Speak with expressiveness and enthusiasm, in a warm, pleasant tone, with pitch variety. Use volume appropriate for the size of the room. Breathe deeply and fully.
- Avoid the common problem of speaking in a dull, robotic monotone that sounds as if you were bored. Do not speak too quietly to be heard or too loudly for the size of the room. Also, watch out for a tendency to end declarative sentences as if they were questions.

Rate: Rate is the speed at which you speak.

- Vary your rate somewhat to avoid droning. Generally, keep it slow enough to be understood but fast enough to maintain energy. Use pauses, or "mental punctuation," before or after a key term, to separate items in a series, or to indicate a major break in thought.
- Watch out for speaking at a monotonous, constant rate. An ineffective rate lacks pauses or variation: if too slow, it may bore your audience; if too fast, it may lose them.

Fillers: Fillers are verbal pauses, such as "uh," "er," "um," and "y'know."

- Give yourself permission to pause, if necessary, during your presentation to collect your thoughts. You don't need to fill the pause with a filler.
- Don't overreact if you notice a few fillers; everybody uses them occasionally. If you diagnose a distracting, habitual overuse of fillers, try asking a colleague to signal you every time you use one.

Enunciation: Enunciation is the clarity of your articulation.

- Pronounce your words clearly and crisply—without mumbling, running words together, leaving out syllables, or dropping final consonants.
- Avoid mumbling, which may be perceived as sounding uneducated or hurried. Avoid running words together—as in "gonna" or "wanna"—which is often associated with talking too fast. Avoid leaving out syllables, as in "guvmint." Finally, avoid dropping final consonants, as in "thousan," "jus," or "goin."

3. Space and objects

Another component of nonverbal communication is the use of space and objects around you. Objects and space affect four sets of choices: seating arrangements, speaker height and distance, use of objects, and dress.

Seating: The way you arrange the chairs for a presentation will communicate nonverbally what kind of interaction you want to have with your audience. Choose straight lines of chairs for the least interactive sessions. Choose horseshoe-shaped or U-shaped lines of chairs to encourage more interaction. For smaller groups choose either (1) a rectangular table, with a person seated at the head, to emphasize the power of the leader, or (2) a round table to encourage equality among participants.

Height and distance: The higher you are in relationship to your audience, the more formal the atmosphere you are establishing nonverbally. Therefore, the most formal presentations might be delivered from a stage or a platform. In a semiformal situation, you stand while your audience sits. To make the situation even less formal, place yourself and your audience at the same level: sit together around a table or seat yourself in front of the group. Similarly, the closer you are, the less formal you appear.

Objects: The more objects you place between yourself and the audience, the more formal the interaction. To increase formality, use a podium, desk, or table between yourself and the audience. To decrease formality, stand or sit without any articles of furniture between you and your audience.

Dress: What you wear also communicates something to your audience. Dress to project the image that you want to create. Dress appropriately for the audience, the occasion, the organization, and the culture. For instance, what is appropriate in the fashion industry may be totally inappropriate in the banking industry. Finally, avoid attire that will distract from what you are saying—such as exaggerated, dangling jewelry or loud, flashy ties.

4. Practice and arrangements

Using the following practice and arrangement techniques will improve your nonverbal delivery.

Practice techniques: Here are some possible practice techniques.

- *Avoid reading or memorizing.* You won't be able to establish eye contact or rapport with your audience if you are reading and you won't have time to memorize every presentation. Therefore, practice speaking conversationally, referring to your note cards as little as you can. (See pages 16–17 for tips on composing note cards.)
- *Rehearse out loud on your feet.* Knowing your content and saying it aloud are two completely different activities, so do not practice by sitting and reading over your note cards. Instead, practice out loud and on your feet. For an important presentation, rehearse the entire thing out loud and on your feet. For a less important presentation, practice the opening, closing, and main transitions this way.
- *Memorize three key parts.* Another suggestion is to memorize your opening, closing, and major transitions. During these times, speakers tend to feel the most nervous and are most apt to lose their composure.
- *Practice with your slides.* Make sure your equipment works and you know how to use it smoothly. Practice integrating what you are saying with what you are showing and avoiding delivery problems such as turning around and talking to the screen or aggressively thrusting the remote at it.
- *Improve your delivery.* While you're practicing, you can work to improve your delivery by videotaping your rehearsal, by practicing in front of a friend or a colleague, or by speaking into a mirror (to improve your facial expression) or an audiotape recorder (to improve your vocal expression).
- *Simulate the situation.* You might try practicing in the actual place where you will be making the presentation or in front of chairs set up as they will be when you speak.
- *Time yourself.* Time yourself in advance to avoid the irritating problem of running overtime during your presentation. You prefer to hear short presentations; so does your audience. During your rehearsal, remember to (1) speak slowly, as you would to actual people, rather than just reading through your slides; (2) speak extra slowly during your preview, to give your audience time to digest it; (3) include time to change and explain your slides; (4) add some extra time for interruptions and questions; and then (5) add in some extra time because the real presentation usually takes 10 to 20 percent longer than the practice version.

Arrangement reminders: Another way to gain confidence is to make the necessary arrangements for your presentation so that you won't be flustered upon discovering your computer doesn't work with the projector provided or you have too few chairs. All the work you do to create a presentation may be wasted if you haven't made such arrangements. Remember that you are responsible for your own arrangements. Although the janitor, your secretary, or the audiovisual technician can help you out, you are the one who will be suffering in front of the audience if arrangements go awry.

You will deliver your presentation more effectively if you do not arrive at the last moment. Get there about 30 minutes early to check the arrangements, fix anything that may be wrong, get comfortable with the place, and mingle with the audience.

- *Room:* First, double-check your room arrangements. Make sure that you have enough chairs, but not too many. Get rid of extras in advance; people don't like to move once they're seated. Make sure that the chairs are arranged as you want them to be and that any other items you ordered are there and functioning. Check the lighting, ventilation, sources of noise, and any other potential distractions. (If, despite your best efforts, a distraction occurs during the presentation, don't get flustered or pretend it's not happening. Deal with it as naturally as you can.)
- *Slides:* Second, check your slide arrangements. Make sure that all the equipment and accessories you ordered have arrived. Test all the equipment far enough in advance so that you can get someone to fix or replace it if necessary. Check the sequence of your slides and handouts. Get the number to call if something should break down during your presentation.

  Test the readability of your slides by viewing them from the farthest chair or asking someone seated in the back row. Make sure that every person in the audience will be able to read your slides. If the room is much larger than you thought it would be and the slides are not readable from the back, try to rearrange the room so the chairs are closer to the screen.
- *Yourself:* Finally, arrange yourself (as it were). Set up your note cards and anything else you might need, such as a glass of water. Remember that you are "on stage" from the moment the first person arrives until the moment you leave the room. Prepare yourself physically and mentally by using one of the specific relaxation techniques described on the following pages.

II. RELAXATION TECHNIQUES

To deliver your best presentation, you need to be so relaxed that the presentation feels like a conversation with the audience. However, when most people present, they feel a surge of adrenaline. In fact, fear of public speaking ranks as Americans' number-one fear—ahead of both death and loneliness. So the trick is to get that adrenaline-based energy working for you instead of against you, by finding an effective relaxation technique. Experiment with the various methods explained on the next six pages until you find the one or two techniques that are most useful for you.

1. Physical relaxation

The first set of relaxation techniques is based on the assumption, shared by many performers and athletes, that by relaxing yourself physically, you will calm yourself mentally.

Exercise: One way to relax is to exercise before a presentation. Many people calm down following the physical exertion of running, working out, or other athletic activities.

Progressive relaxation: Developed by psychologist Edmund Jacobson, this technique involves tensing and relaxing muscle groups. To practice this technique, set aside about 10 to 15 minutes of undisturbed time in a comfortable, darkened place where you can lie down. Tense (by clenching vigorously for 5 to 7 seconds) and relax (by releasing and enjoying the feeling for at least 10 seconds) each muscle group in turn: face, neck and chest, arms and hands, chest and upper back, stomach and lower back, upper legs, lower legs, and feet. Repeat the procedure at least twice.

Deep breathing: For at least one full minute, sit or lie on your back with your hand on your diaphragm, just below the rib cage.

- *Yoga "sigh breath":* Inhale slowly through your nose to the count of four, feeling your diaphragm expand. Exhale even more slowly through your mouth feeling your diaphragm empty—to the count of six to eight, or counting backwards from four—and sighing aloud.
- *Sarnoff squeeze:* Similarly, speech coach Dorothy Sarnoff recommends inhaling through your nose and exhaling through your mouth, making a "sssss" sound and contracting the abdominus rectus muscles, what she calls the "vital triangle" just below the rib cage.

Specific body parts: For some people, stage fright manifests itself in certain parts of the body—for example, tensed shoulders, quivering arms, or fidgety hands. Here are some exercises to relax specific body parts.

- *Neck and throat:* Gently roll your neck from side to side, front to back, chin to chest, or all the way around.
- *Shoulders:* Raise one or both shoulders as if you were shrugging. Then roll them back, then down, then forward. After several repetitions, rotate in the opposite direction.
- *Arms:* Shake out your arms, first only at the shoulders, then only at the elbow, finally letting your hands flop at the wrist.
- *Hands:* Repeatedly clench and relax your fists. Start with an open hand and close each finger one by one to make a fist; hold the clench; then release.
- *Face:* Close your eyes and wiggle your face muscles: forehead, nose, cheeks, and jaws. Move your jaw side-to-side.

Vocal relaxation: Some nervous symptoms affect your voice—such as quivering, dry mouth, or sounding out-of-breath. Here are some general suggestions for keeping your voice in shape:

- *Be awake and rested:* Get enough sleep the night before you speak, so your voice will be rested. Wake up several hours before your presentation to provide a natural warm-up period for your voice.
- *Take a hot shower:* A hot shower will wake up your voice; the steam will soothe a tired or irritated set of vocal cords.
- *Drink warm liquids:* Ideal candidates are herbal tea and warm water with lemon. Warm liquids with caffeine are fine for your voice, but they might increase your heart rate.
- *Avoid consuming milk* or other dairy products. Dairy products tend to coat the vocal cords, which may cause problems during your presentation.
- *Avoid dry mouth* by sucking a cough drop or hard candy, chewing gum, or gently biting the end of your tongue before the presentation.
- *Hum* to warm up your voice. Start slowly and quietly, gradually adding a full range of pitches.
- *During the presentation:* (1) *Drink water:* Keep water nearby. If you have dry mouth, pause and drink as needed. (2) *Breathe deeply* from the diaphragm (below the rib cage), not shallowly from the shoulders or upper chest.

2. Mental relaxation

Some speakers prefer mental relaxation techniques that control physical sensation mentally. Here are various mental relaxation techniques to try until you find one that works for you.

Think positively. Base your thinking on the Dale Carnegie argument: To feel brave, act as if you are brave. To feel confident, act as if you are confident.

Repeat positive words or phrases. Fill your mind with positive words or phrases, such as "poised, perfect, prepared, poised, perfect, prepared."

Think nonjudgmentally. Describe your behavior ("I notice a monotone") rather than judging it ("I have a terrible speaking voice!"). Then change the behavior by thinking rationally or using a positive self-picture, both of which are described next.

Think rationally. Avoid being trapped in the "ABCs of emotional reactions," as developed by psychologist Albert Ellis. **A** stands for the "activating event" (such as catching yourself using a filler word), which sparks an irrational **B** or "belief system" (such as "I must be absolutely perfect in every way; if I'm not perfect, then I must be terrible"), which causes **C** or "consequences" (such as anxiety or depression). Ellis recommends **D** or "disputing" these ABCs with a rational thought (such as "I don't demand absolute perfection from other speakers" or "Using one filler word is not the end of the world. I'll go on naturally instead of getting flustered").

Use a positive self-picture. Many speakers find that positive self-pictures work better than positive words.

- *Visualize yourself as a successful speaker,* including hearing positive comments or applause. Act out this visualization in your head. Then act out the role of the person you've been visualizing.
- *Use a positive video picture:* Work with a videotape of yourself giving a real or simulated presentation. Freeze the video at the point where you really like yourself, where you look and sound strong. Then carry that picture around in your head. When it's time for the next presentation, recreate that person.

- *Think of yourself as the guru.* Remind yourself that you know your subject matter.
- *Put yourself "in character"* of a professional speaker by your comportment and dress.

Don't think. (1) *While you are waiting to speak,* fill your mind with something mindless, like saying the alphabet. (2) *While you are speaking,* turn off your internal self-analysis and don't think about how you look or sound.

Try visualization. Relax by conjuring up in your mind a visual image of a positive and pleasant object or scene.

- *Imagine a scene:* On each of the several days before the presentation, close your eyes and imagine a beautiful, calm scene, such as a beach you have visited. Imagine the details of temperature, color, and fragrance. If your mind wanders, bring it back to your scene. Concentrate on the image and exclude all else. Try repeating positive phrases, such as "I feel warm and relaxed" or "I feel content."
- *Juxtapose the stress:* A few days before the presentation, visualize the room, the people, and the stresses. Then distance yourself and relax by visualizing this pleasant image. This technique decreases stress by defusing the situation in your mind.

Connect with the audience. Try to see your audience as real people.

- *Meet them and greet them:* When people are arriving, greet them and get to know some of them. Then, when you're speaking, find those people in the audience and feel as if you're having a one-to-one conversation with them.
- *Remember they are individuals:* Even if you can't greet the people in the audience, think of them as individual people, not as an amorphous audience. As you speak, imagine you are conversing with them.
- *"Befriend" the audience:* Picture yourself in your own home, talking enthusiastically with old friends. Try to maintain a sense of warmth and goodwill. In addition to diffusing your anxiety, this altered perception can also increase your positive energy.

Transform negative to positive. Consider the adrenaline that may be causing nervous symptoms as a positive energy. All speakers may feel butterflies in their stomachs; effective speakers get those butterflies to fly in formation, thereby transforming negative energy into positive energy.

3. Last-minute relaxation

When it's actually time to deliver the presentation, here are a few relaxation techniques that you can use at the last minute—and even as you speak.

Last-minute physical relaxation: Obviously, you cannot start doing push-ups or practice humming as you're sitting or standing there, about ready to begin speaking. Fortunately, however, you can use other techniques to relax your body at the last minute—techniques no one can see you using.

- *Isometric exercises:* Clench and then quickly relax your muscles. For example, you might press or wiggle your feet against the floor, one hand against your other hand, or your hands against the table or chair; you might clench your fists, thighs, or toes. Then quickly relax the muscles you just clenched.
- *Deep breathing exercises:* Inhale slowly and deeply from the diaphragm, then exhale slowly and completely. Pause between breaths. Try breathing in through your nose and out through your mouth. Or, try imagining you are breathing in "the good" and breathing out "the bad." Avoid hyperventilating or shallow breathing from your upper chest.

Last-minute mental relaxation: Also at the last minute, you may dispel stage fright mentally by using what behavioral psychologists call "internal dialogue," which means, of course, talking to yourself. Here are some examples:

- *Give yourself a pep talk:* "What I am about to say is important" or "I am ready" or "They are just people."
- *Play up your audience's reception:* "They are interested in my topic" or "They are a friendly group of people."
- *Repeat positive phrases:* "I'm glad I'm here; I'm glad you're here" or "I know I know" or "I care about you."

As you speak: Finally, here are four techniques that you can use to relax even as you speak.

- *Speak to the "motivational listeners."* Every audience always includes a few kind souls who nod, smile, and generally react favorably. Especially at the beginning of your presentation, look at them, not at the people reading, looking out the window, or yawning. Looking at positive listeners will increase your confidence. Soon you will be looking at the people around those good listeners and ultimately at every person in the audience.
- *Talk to someone in the back row.* At the beginning of the presentation, take a deep breath and talk to the person in the back row to force breathing and volume.
- *Remember that you probably look better than you think you do.* Your nervousness is probably not as apparent to your audience as it is to you. Experiments show that even trained speech instructors do not see all the nervous symptoms speakers think they are exhibiting. We hear managers and students watching videotapes of their performances regularly say, "Hey, I look better than I thought I would!"
- *Concentrate on the here and now.* Focus on your ideas and your audience. Forget about past regrets and future uncertainties. You have already analyzed what to do: now just do it wholeheartedly. Enjoy communicating your information to your audience, and let your enthusiasm show.

CHAPTER OUTLINE

I. BEFORE PRESENTATION DAY
   1. Check your slides.
   2. Practice your slide interaction.
   3. Consider using handouts.
   4. Create your handouts.

II. ON PRESENTATION DAY
   1. Getting set up
   2. Solving projection problems

CHAPTER 11

PowerPoint Delivery

In addition to paying attention to the general nonverbal aspects of presenting, keep in mind the additional delivery issues associated with using PowerPoint—both before and on the day of your presentation.

I. BEFORE PRESENTATION DAY

Good PowerPoint delivery begins before you start to speak—and includes (1) checking your slides, (2) practicing your slide interaction, (3) considering the use of handouts, and (4) creating handouts.

1. Check your slides.

After you complete your slides, and preferably the next day or at least after a break, be sure to check over those slides one last time.

Check the accuracy of facts. Double-check any fact or statistic that you include in your presentation. If necessary, go back to the original research and check that no transposition errors occurred. If you are using a startling or controversial item, double-check the source to make sure you recorded it correctly when making your original notes.

Check the consistency among your outline, note cards, and slides. Without really knowing it, many times when we develop our slides we end up modifying our points as we try to make the slides look good. Go back to your original outline and to your note cards and make sure that they are all true to one another.

Check the message/slide connection. Make sure that . . .

- All of your slides have message titles, as explained on pages 23–24.
- All graphic elements, including photos and videos, reinforce the message you are making on the slide. Honestly review each one to make sure that you are not including a graphic for its own sake.
- All charts and diagrams are correct for the point you want to make and you have added color emphasis only where appropriate.

Recheck spelling and grammar. Unfortunately, spelling and grammar mistakes are a common problem. These mistakes—magnified on screen—may decrease your credibility despite all the careful analysis that went into your presentation. Check every word in your slides yourself, not relying only on spell check, as explained in the guidelines on page 102.

Run through in presentation mode. Switch into presentation mode and run through the entire presentation slide by slide.

- Choose from any of three ways to switch into presentation mode. (1) Press the F5 key on any slide to start the presentation from the first slide. (2) Click on the Slide Show button ❶ in the lower left corner of the screen to start the slide show from the slide you are currently editing. (This button looks like a small screen; it is the one on the right of the three buttons for editing, slide sorter mode, and slide show mode.) (3) Click Slide Show → View Show.
- Check that your bullets and subpoints and your graphics all build on the slide the way you want them to—either one-by-one, in subgroups, or all at once.
- Make sure the text animation is set to Appear rather than to a distracting animation such as Dissolve in or Checkerboard. (See pages 106–107 for instructions.)
- Make sure that the transition between slides is set to No Transition instead of a distracting transition such as Newsflash or Wheel Clockwise.
- Check that each tracker is set properly. (See pages 55–57 for instructions.)

Prepare extra slides for Q&A (optional). If you expect questions and answers during or after your presentation, you might want to prepare some extra slides in anticipation of possible questions. Insert these slides at the end of your slideshow. If one of these questions comes up, you can switch to the Q&A slide, using the instructions on page 155, for moving to any slide in the show.

Create several copies of your summary slide at the end of the presentation to prevent an extra click on the remote sending you back into the program. This tactic makes sure that the last slide the audience sees is the summary slide. It is a good idea to leave your summary slide displayed at the end of the presentation and during questions and answers, to reinforce your main take-aways in your audience's minds.

Insert a black slide at the end of the presentation. As the audience is leaving the room, display a black slide so that they do not glance up and see the presentation drop into the operating system screen.

- Click Tools → Options → View tab.
- Set End with black slide option ❶.

Make a slide reference list. Make a list of the slide numbers and titles so that you will always know where you are in the presentation.

- Click Outline tab ❶.
- Click View → Toolbars → Outlining.

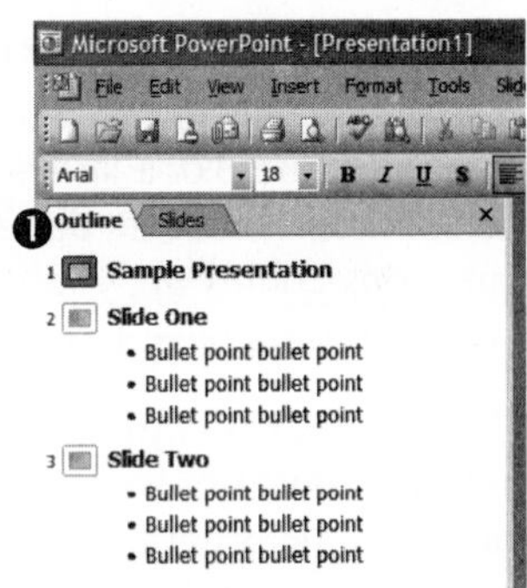

• Click the Collapse All button ❷.

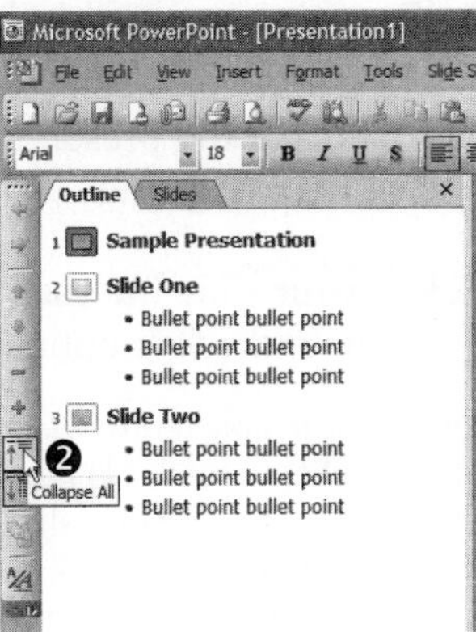

• Click File → Print.
• Select Outline View ❶ → Click OK.

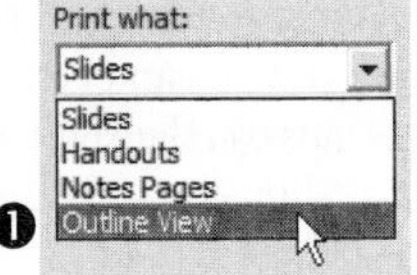

In addition to checking your slides, we also recommend that you order a remote to advance and reverse your slides. The remote is far more graceful and less obtrusive than using the keyboard, because you can move anywhere you wish and you don't have to look down at the keyboard.

2. Practice your slide interaction.

Think about what equipment you will use to interact with your slides during the presentation and then practice with the equipment you have chosen.

Select your slide interaction options. Here are our recommendations about the four options you have available.

- *Use a remote if possible:* Order a remote or bring one of your own if possible because (1) it is the most graceful and least obtrusive way to advance and reverse slides; (2) you can move anywhere you wish and you don't have to look down at the keyboard; and (3) it is extremely easy to use by pressing the forward key to advance or the back key to reverse.
- *Use the keyboard if necessary:* Using the keyboard restricts your movement and breaks your eye contact. However, if you need to use it, you can (1) advance slides by pressing any of four keys: the down arrow, the right arrow, the Page Down, or the N key; and (2) reverse slides by pressing any of four keys: the up arrow, the left arrow, the Page Up, or the P key.
- *Do not use the mouse.* We recommend against using the mouse. The mouse works easily only to left-click to advance slides. If you right-click to reverse slides, however, a submenu with options appears, which looks unattractive and unprofessional. Finally, you always need to hide the cursor if you use the mouse by pressing Ctrl+H.
- *Do not use a laser pointer.* We also recommend against using a laser pointer. The dot created by the laser pointer is extremely small and hard to see. Also, most presenters can't hold the pointer perfectly still, causing the dot to jiggle around on the screen. Instead, we recommend inserting an emphatic arrow or circle on the slide that you can show as part of your click sequence.

Practice with your equipment. Whatever you choose to use, however, be sure to practice with it in advance until you can use it without thinking. In addition to practicing advancing and reversing slides, keep in mind the following:

To move to any slide in the show:

- Type in the slide number (using the number keys on the keyboard) → Press Enter.

To allow the audience time to read each point:

- As each bullet point of text is displayed on the screen, remember to pause for a second or two to give the audience time to read what just appeared on the screen and return their focus to what you are about to say.

To toggle between the slide and a black screen:

- *Keyboard:* Press the B key (each press toggles between a black screen and the slide you are on).
- *Remote:* Click the blank screen key.

To toggle between showing the cursor arrow and hiding it:

- Press the A key (each press toggles between showing and hiding the cursor arrow).
- Be aware that the cursor arrow may appear if you move the mouse or move the pointer control on a remote that has mouse features.

To draw on the screen during the show:

- Hold the Ctrl key down and press the P key to turn the cursor into a pen → Drag the pen to draw lines → Press E to erase what you have drawn (optional) → Hold the Ctrl key down and press the A key to return the cursor to the arrow cursor → Press A to hide the cursor.

To end the show:

- Press the Escape key (labeled "Esc" on the keyboard).

3. Consider using handouts.

One of the biggest disadvantages of oral presentations is that, unlike written documents, they don't provide a permanent record. For this reason, many presenters provide hard copy of their slides as handouts. The following section explains the kinds of handouts, their advantages and disadvantages, and when and how to use them.

Three kinds of handouts: Three prevalent ways of providing hard copy include:

- *Deck presentations:* Deck presentations are bound 8½ by 11 inch copies of your slides. Decks can range from being professionally bound and printed in color to being simply stapled and printed in black and white. Sometimes decks provide a copy of the projected visuals; other times, they are used alone, with the presenter talking about each page in turn.

  Deck presentations can be useful for several reasons. First, they allow you to be more interactive because you and the audience follow the presentation together. Second, they allow you to change the environment, setting, or lighting of a slide show. Finally, you can use them as "leave-behinds" that may contain supporting text and background data that didn't appear in the slide show.

  If you use a deck, keep these suggestions in mind. Always insert a page number on each page, so you can refer your audience to the right spot. Also, remember that wire-bound versions are easier to flip than those that are taped or stapled.
- *Slide copies:* Another option, less formal than a deck, is to provide copies of your slides, printed either two, three, or four per page.
- *Specific handouts:* Some handouts provide detailed information to augment your visual aids in a specific section of your presentation, such as financial data or spreadsheets.

Advantages of handouts: In general, hard copy enhances . . .

- *Audience recall:* Handouts give people something to which they can refer later. For example, in a sales situation, you might want them to have a document to convince others to purchase your product or service; in a training situation, you want them to have a document to use for reference.
- *Audience attention:* Your audience can pay more attention to what you are saying because they don't need to frantically copy down your slides.

- *More relevant note taking:* Your handout allows audience members to take notes on those parts of your message that are most relevant to them or their situation.
- *Audience interaction:* If you number your slide handout pages, you can refer to a certain page by number.
- *Ability to reach more people:* People who did not attend your presentation can read the hard copy; therefore, stand-alone sense becomes even more important.
- *Branding:* By including your presentation title and name in the handout header and a copyright notice and contact information in the handout footer, you can reinforce your brand and allow people to contact you later with questions.
- *A backup if the equipment fails:* If your equipment fails, you can still proceed with your presentation using the handouts as the guide. Make sure that you have a copy of the handout yourself in case you suddenly need to use it.

Disadvantages of handouts: Although hard copy has many advantages, be sure to keep in mind how to overcome the following disadvantages.

- *Keep your audience with you:* The main disadvantage of hard copy is that your audience can read ahead and become distracted from what you are saying. Therefore, be sure to not hand out your speaking notes or a transcript, which may become a substitute for the audience listening to you.
- *Avoid reading:* Do not lose your eye contact and interaction with your audience by reading the handouts aloud. Look at your audience, not at the handouts.
- *Avoid overloading:* Your handouts should be copies of your slides; therefore, they should contain your main ideas only, not a word-for-word script.
- *Stay flexible:* Hard copy, once printed, cannot be changed the way slides can. Therefore, remember that you should be responsive to your audience: for example, omit pages that turn out to be unnecessary, change the sequence of pages, or jump ahead if appropriate.

When to use handouts: You may distribute your handouts (1) *before the presentation* if you want your audience to prepare in advance for a discussion, (2) *during the presentation* so they can take notes, or (3) *after the presentation* if you don't want them to read ahead of what you are saying.

In general, we recommend distributing handouts during the presentation so (1) they can avoid trying to write down what they see on your slides, and (2) you can refer them to your handout (for example, "As you can see on page 6 . . .").

How to design and print hard copy:

- *Decks:* Create a deck by printing your slides one slide-per-page. Decks can range from being professionally bound and printed in color to being simply stapled and printed in black and white. If you use a deck, always insert a page number on each page, so you can refer your audience to the right spot ("As you can see on page 9 . . .").
- *Slide copies:* PowerPoint offers several design options for creating slide copies. From best to worse they are: (1) four slides-per-page, which has the most unlined white space on each page so audience members can write wherever they want; (2) one or two slides-per-page, which generates too much paper and leaves little room for notes; (3) three slides-per-page with lines, which makes your audience write on the lines instead of around the slides; and (4) six or nine slides-per-page, which lacks enough space for notes.
- *Specific handouts:* You can also create specific handouts using any software, including Word for text documents or Excel for spreadsheets. Include page numbers on these handouts so you can refer to them during the presentation if necessary.

How to present with decks:

- *Preview the purpose:* Tell the audience the purpose of the deck and how you will be using it during the presentation. Do you want them to read it in advance, during, or after the presentation?
- *Give direction:* Direct the audience to the specific page you are discussing ("As you can see on page 12 . . .", "On the next four pages . . .").
- *Point out key items:* Introduce each new page: explain your color coding ("As you see, the green trend line represents . . ."), the chart elements ("Across the top of the matrix, we have listed the criteria . . . Down the side, we have identified the job candidates . . ."); and point out the main message ("Note that the trend is . . ." "Contrast the . . . with the . . .").
- *Don't read from the deck:* Talk to the audience, not the paper. If possible, put the deck on a table so you can gesture, and be sure to look up so you can make eye contact.
- *Be responsive:* Remember that deck presentations are supposed to be flexible and interactive. Be responsive to your audience: for example, omit pages that turn out to be unnecessary, change the sequence of pages, or jump ahead if appropriate.

4. Create your handouts.

To create a consistent look for each handout page, first set up the Handout Master. When printing your handouts, you can select which slides are to be included in the handout if you do not want to use them all.

Composing your handouts:

- *To open the Handout Master:*

  —Click View → Master → Handout Master.

  —In the row of toolbar buttons that show the different handout formats (from one-per-page through nine-per-page), select the four-per-page handout format ❶.

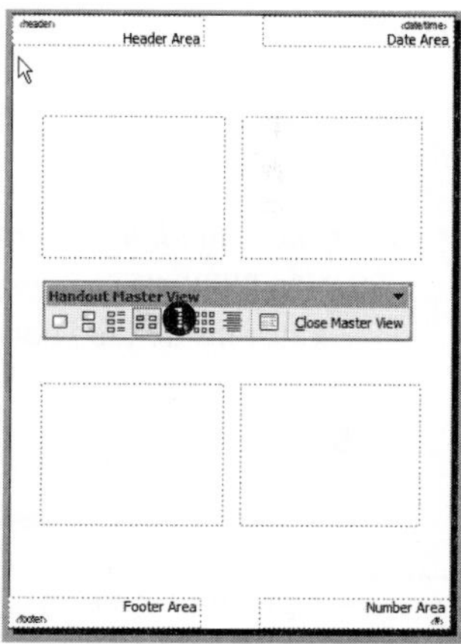

- *To create a handout header* that will appear on the top line of each page of your handout:
  - —Click inside the Header Area ❷ → Enter text.
  - —*Optional:* Choose a header text font using the instructions on page 45. Use a 10-point font size so it won't draw too much attention to itself.

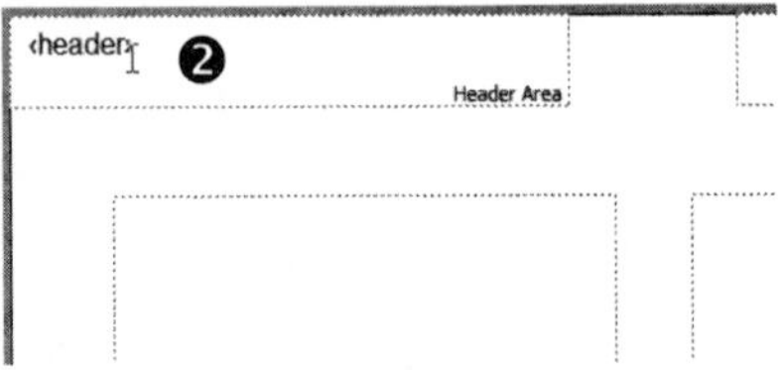

- *To create a handout footer* (for copyright information, disclaimers, and page numbers):
  - —Click inside the Footer Area ❶ → Enter text.

  - —*Optional:* Choose a footer text font using instructions on page 45.
  - —Click inside the Number Area ❷ → Enter text before the <#> symbol representing the page number.
  - —*Optional:* Use a 10-point font size so it won't draw too much attention to itself.

- *To close the Handout Master:*
  - —Click Close Master View ❶.

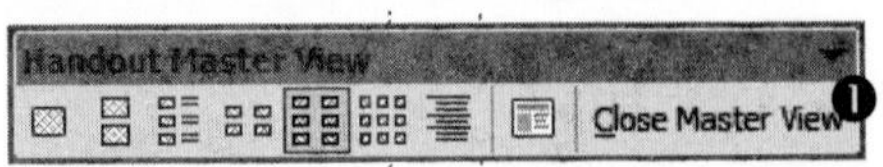

Printing your handouts:

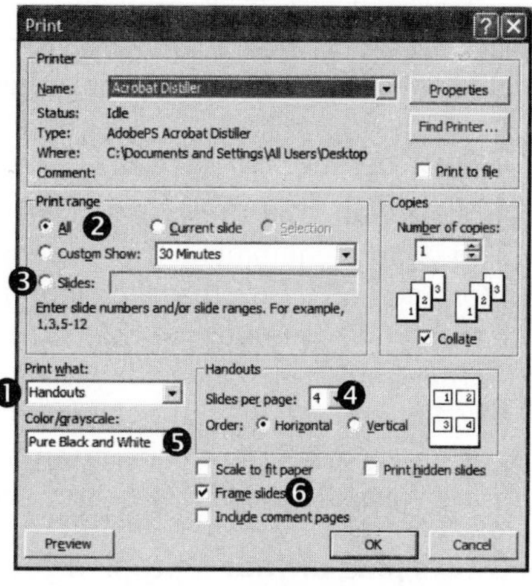

- Click File → Print.
- Select Handouts to print ❶.
- Select which slides to print ❷, usually All.

  Optional: If you don't want to print all of them, select the Slides button ❸ and enter the numbers of the slides you want included:
  (1) Use a hyphen between the numbers to indicate a consecutive range of slides (e.g., for 1 through 10, enter 1-10);
  (2) Use a comma between the numbers to indicate slides not in a consecutive range (e.g., for 2 and 12, enter 2,12); (3) You can combine hyphens and commas (e.g., 1,2,6-10,12).
- Usually select 4 slides-per-page ❹. Select 1 slide-per-page if you are printing a deck.
- Select Pure Black and White printing for black and white printers ❺.
- Select Frame slides ❻.

II. ON PRESENTATION DAY

Here are some tips to enhance your PowerPoint interaction and delivery before and during your presentation.

1. Getting set up

On the day of your presentation, arrive early to the room and set up all of your equipment. Connect your computer to the data projector and make sure that the data projector is started before you turn on your computer so that the computer recognizes that an external display is connected.

After you set up your equipment and start your computer, but before you switch into presentation mode, check these items to ensure you will have a trouble-free presentation.

Always plug in your laptop. If you are presenting from a laptop computer, make sure it is plugged in, not running on battery power. You will undermine your credibility if a low battery warning pops up in the middle of the presentation and you have to scramble to plug the power cord in.

Run your presentation from the hard drive. If you are using a memory drive or CD instead of your own computer, make sure you copy the presentation files to the hard drive of the computer you will be using. Your slides will advance much more quickly if they are on a hard drive than if they are on a memory drive or CD.

Check the projection. If the room is equipped with an LCD or plasma flat panel, you will find that the slides look much brighter and the colors much truer than on a data projector. If the room is equipped with a data projector, however, be aware that the colors will probably not look exactly the same as they did on your desktop or laptop computer monitor. So, double-check the colors and adjust them if necessary.

Turn off screen savers. Before you deliver your presentation, use the display options of your operating system (such as Windows XP) to make sure that all screen savers are turned off. Having a screen saver pop up in the middle of an important point in your presentation looks amateurish and annoying.

Turn off the power saving mode. Another audience irritant occurs if the screen suddenly goes blank during the presentation. To avoid such an occurrence, use the power saving options of the operating system to turn off all power saving modes that blank the screen after a set number of minutes.

Adjust poor screen lighting. The image you see displayed on the screen may look washed out if lights are directly above or pointed towards the screen. In this case . . .

- Turn off the lights directly above the screen, unless doing so makes the room too dim.
- If you can't turn off the lights or if turning them off makes the room too dim, you may want to ask the maintenance staff on site to unscrew a few of the most offending lightbulbs.

Check for a weak projector or bulb. If the image on the screen is so dim that you can't see it until the lights are completely turned off, check for the following two problems. If neither can be fixed, your only option is to dim more of the lights in the room to make the image seem brighter.

- *The projector:* Ask the technical staff if the projector has a brightness rating of under 1,000 lumens. In this case, try to get a new projector because projectors rated fewer than 1,000 lumens are usually only bright enough in small rooms with minimal lighting.
- *The bulb:* Old bulbs will project a dim image because, unlike other bulbs, they do not go out suddenly, but gradually. To check to see whether you have a bulb problem, ask the technical staff to find out how many hours the bulb has been used by checking the bulb usage option on the projector screen menu. A bulb over half of its rate life (usually 1,000–2,000 hours) will probably be too dim. If you cannot get a new projector, the only solution is to replace the bulb. Unfortunately, bulbs are so expensive that extras are not usually on site, and even if they are, you need to wait until the projector has cooled down enough to handle the old bulb.

Match the projector and computer resolution. If your computer's display resolution is higher than that of the projector, the quality of the image may be very low. This problem occurs because the projector will adjust the image down to the resolution that it can display by dropping lines out of the higher-resolution image.

To solve this problem . . .

- *Adjust the resolution on your computer.* You can adjust the resolution of your computer to match that of the projector by using the display settings in the computer's operating system.
- *Get a new projector.* Another option, if you have time, is to get a new projector that has the same resolution as the computer.

Check your remote. Check your remote batteries to make sure they are working.

Check your microphone if you're using one: (1) Test the sound to check your volume. (2) Test to see whether your distance from the microphone affects your volume. For unidirectional microphones (like those attached to a lectern), you must keep your distance (which can vary from 2 to 20 inches) constant. Avoid unwanted sounds: breathe quietly and avoid rattling papers, drumming your fingers, and jingling coins.

2. Solving projection problems

Most of your PowerPoint presentations will be delivered by hooking up a computer to a data projector and projecting your slides onto a screen. If everything is connected yet the image does not display on the screen or is fuzzy or blurry, check these common problems:

Plug in the projector. Incredible as it seems, lack of power to the projector is a common problem. Make sure that (1) the projector cord is plugged into the the wall, (2) the power bar is turned on. Check that the power cord is in the wall outlet if the data projector does not turn on. Also, if you are using a power bar, check that its switch has been turned on.

Tighten cable connections. Loose cables between the computer and data projector also account for a remarkable number of display problems. Make sure all cables are securely connected to the appropriate port with the thumbscrews used to secure each end of the cable to the port on the equipment.

Take the projector out of standby mode. If you plug your computer into a projector that someone else has just been using and your display does not come up, check the projector's standby mode.

Set display mode. You have a choice among three display modes: laptop only, screen only (through the external video port), or both at once. To choose among the three modes, press the following two keys simultaneously: (1) a key (usually one of the function keys) that has a picture of a display (looks like a rounded rectangle representing a screen shape) or the letters VGA or CRT on it, and (2) a special Function key (usually labeled Fn). After you press these two keys, wait at least 5 to 10 seconds for the new setting to take effect. Each time you press the key combination, the system switches to the next mode in the cycle of three modes.

Set the projector input source to the computer. From the button on the top of the projector, choose the computer input (rather than the video or other inputs). You may have to go into the projector menu to change the input source on some older projectors.

PART V

Glossaries

GLOSSARY 1	Basic Instructions For the PowerPoint Novice
GLOSSARY 2	PowerPoint Terms and Shortcuts For the "How To Do It" Sections
GLOSSARY 3	Design and Editing Terms For the "What To Do" Sections

GLOSSARY I

Basic Instructions

For the PowerPoint Novice

Never used PowerPoint? No problem. This glossary will explain (1) the screen view that you'll see when you open PowerPoint, (2) the basic terms used in our instructions, and (3) the basic file operations you will use.

Please note that these instructions are for Windows users (in PowerPoint 2002 or PowerPoint 2003). Mac users will find some differences in their version.

OPENING SCREEN VIEW

When you open PowerPoint, you will see a screen that looks like this:

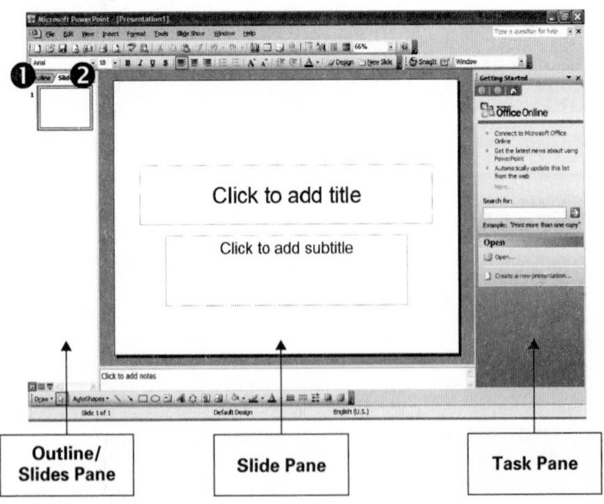

The screen is divided into three sections, called panes:

1. **The Outline/Slides Pane,** on the left side of the screen, allows you to see your entire presentation in either of two ways, by choosing between the two tabs at the top of the pane: the Outline tab ❶ and the Slides tab ❷.

- *The Outline tab* shows you just the words on each slide. Use this option to check the flow of your ideas without being distracted by the graphical appearance or to move text between slides to improve your structure.
- *The Slides tab* shows you a thumbnail (small graphical representation) of each slide the way it will look on screen. Use this option when you want to find a slide quickly.

2. **The Slide Pane,** at the center of the screen, is where you will spend most of your time. You will compose and edit your slides in this area.

3. **The Task Pane,** on the right side of the screen, will change based on the task you are currently working on.

- On the opening screen view, you see choices to access the PowerPoint help system or open a new or existing file.
- However, when you are performing other tasks, the contents of the Task Pane will change. Examples of task panes that will appear include Slide Layout, Custom Animation, and Clip Art.

BASIC TERMINOLOGY

Here are the basic terms you will see in our instructions.

→: This arrow indicates instructions for you to do in sequence. Sometimes, each instruction starts with a verb, such as:

> Click on the data label → Right-click the data label sub-menu → Click Format Data Labels.

However, if the action doesn't change, we don't repeat the verb each time. For example, the following means click Chart, then click Chart Options, then click Gridlines tab.

> Click Chart → Chart Options → Gridlines tab.

Click: Click the left mouse button.

Double-click: Click the left mouse button twice.

Drag: Hold down the left mouse button while you are moving the mouse.

Enter: Type in text.

Highlight: Select text by clicking the mouse at the start of the text and dragging to the end of the text. The text will then be highlighted in a different shade.

Position: Place the cursor over an item.

Right-click: Click the right mouse button.

Select: Choose an item.

Set: Select an option.

BASIC FILE OPERATIONS

Here are the operations you will be using.

To create a new presentation file:

- Click File → New.
- From the Task Pane at the right of the screen, choose Create a new presentation.

To open an existing file:

- Click File → Open or select Open from the Task Pane.
- Select the file → Click OK.

To save a file:

- Click File → Save.

To close a file:

- Click File → Close. (Save the file before closing if prompted.)

GLOSSARY 2

PowerPoint Terms and Shortcuts

For the "How To Do It" Sections

This glossary explains PowerPoint terms and shortcuts. (If you are a novice PowerPoint user, please see Glossary 1 before you read this one.)

Animation: The way in which each element (such as each line of text or each photograph) appears on the slide during the presentation, used to "build" each element as you present it, so you can discuss each one separately. We recommend using the "Appear" animation effect because it is the most simple and the least distracting (discussed on page 87). See also "Click sequence."

Case: Different choices for capitalization: (1) sentence case (with only the first letter of the first word capitalized, as you would write a sentence), (2) title case (with the first letter of every word capitalized, as you would write a book title, (3) uppercase (with all letters capitalized), and (4) lowercase (nothing capitalized)—discussed on page 43.

Chart area: The space within the body placeholder (explained on page 51) that includes the chart—along with its legend, data labels, axes, etc.—as shown in the dashed-line box around the bad example on the facing page. (We recommend against using legends, as explained on page 70.) Other elements of the slide, such as the title and footers, will appear outside of the chart area.

Chart area (with an ineffective chart inside it)

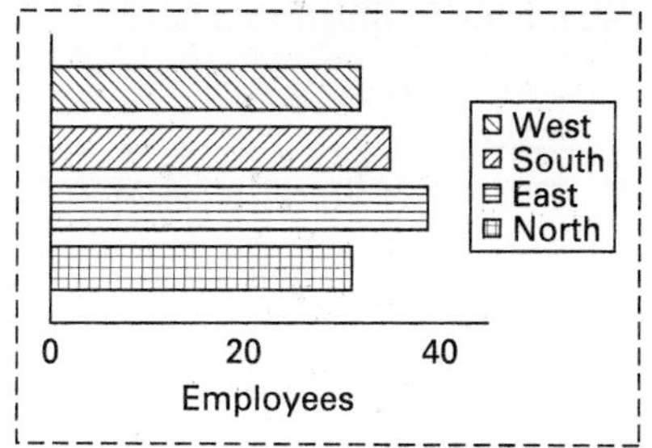

Chart element: Any element within the chart area, including the chart—along with its legend, data labels, axes, and so on. In other words, any element within the preceding dashed-line box.

Chart object: A chart imported from Excel.

Checkbox: A small square that can be checked (selected) or unchecked (not selected) to choose options.

- [x] Clip Art
- [ ] Photographs
- [ ] Movies
- [ ] Sounds

Click sequence: The sequence in which elements (e.g., text, shapes, charts, photographs, etc.) appear on the slide during the presentation each time you click the remote, mouse, or the appropriate key.

Crop: To cut out a part of an item (e.g., a photograph or Clip Art) from any side or corner.

Data labels: Text on the chart that identifies the value or description (such as 28% or Division A) of each data point on a line, each slice in a pie chart, each column in a column chart, etc.

Data series: The set of numbers you use to create a chart, such as the sales percentages, as illustrated here:

Data series

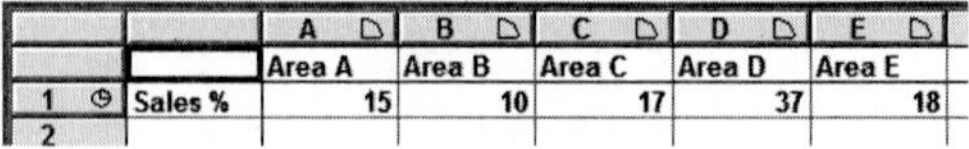

		A	B	C	D	E
		Area A	Area B	Area C	Area D	Area E
1	Sales %	15	10	17	37	18
2						

Resulting pie chart

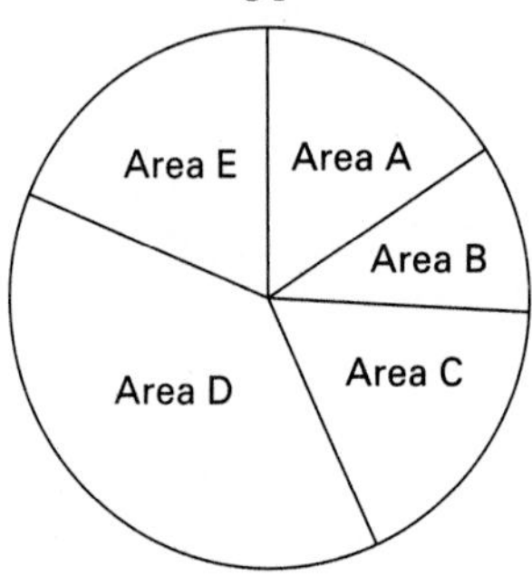

Deck: A presentation shown as a hard-copy printout, not on screen (discussed on pages 156–158).

Distribute: To align items or shapes either vertically or horizontally.

Poorly distributed shapes

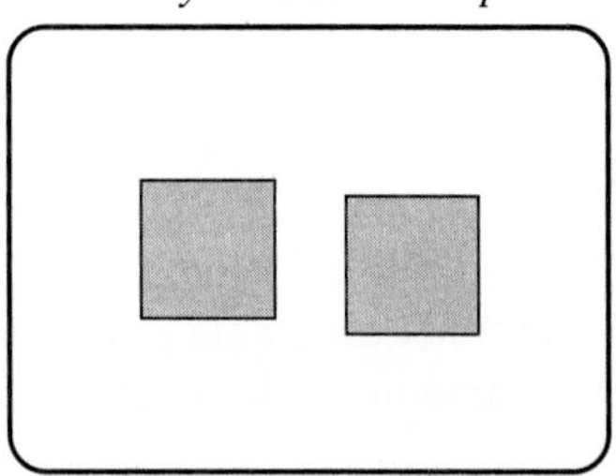

Properly distributed shapes

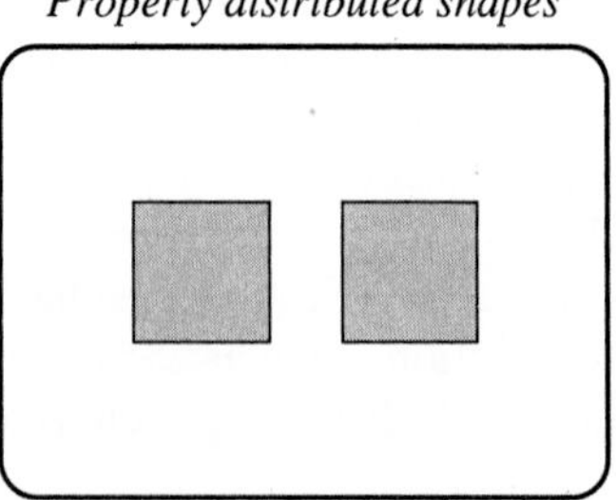

Drawing cursor: A cursor that looks like a plus sign or a set of crosshairs, used to draw a shape.

Regular arrow cursor *Drawing cursor*

Enhanced metafile: A graphic file format to import a chart from Excel so that the chart can be broken apart in PowerPoint and each different part modified later.

Font: The kind of typeface, such as Times New Roman or Arial.

Font effects: Font options, such as shadow or embossed; generally not recommended.

Font size: The size of each letter, measured in points, such as 24 point text.

Font style: Font options, such as regular, bold, or italics.

Height/width ratio (also known as aspect ratio): The ratio of the width to the height of an object. You will need to maintain the height/width ratio when modifying shapes or photographs so they do not get distorted (discussed on page 114).

Proper height/width ratio

Distorted height/width ratio

Pane: A section of the screen, analogous to a pane in a window, each of which is used for a different purpose. The following example shows the three panes on the opening screen.

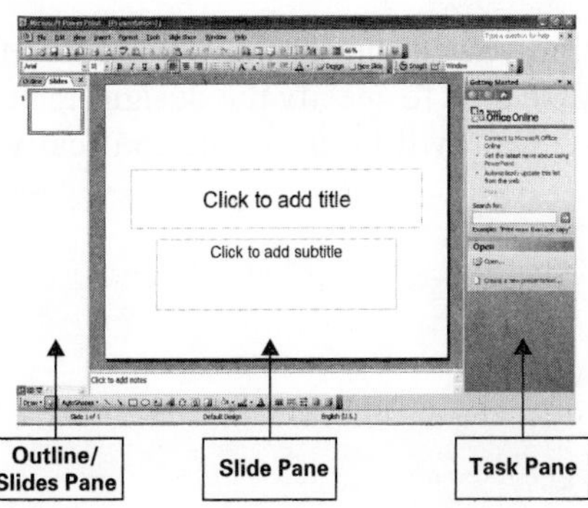

Pixel: A single dot on your computer screen; a typical screen displays XGA resolution of 1024 pixels wide by 768 pixels tall (discussed on page 114).

Placeholder: An area defined on the Slide Master to demarcate a consistent place on the slide for the title, body text, date, footer, and number. The example below shows the locations of five placeholders in the Master Slide (discussed on pages 51–52):

Slide Master

- ❶ *Title:* Where the title will appear
- ❷ *Body text:* Where the bulleted text will appear
- ❸ *Date:* Where you can enter the date or other text
- ❹ *Footer:* Where you can enter a tracker or other text
- ❺ *Number:* Where you can enter the slide number or other text

When you design your Slide Master (the topic of Chapters 3, 4, and 5), you will be able to specify the design (including font style, size, color, etc.) that will be used automatically in all of these placeholders.

Plot area: The space that includes only the chart (e.g., pie, bar, column, etc.) itself, as shown in the dashed-line box around the following bad example.

Bad example: uses a legend

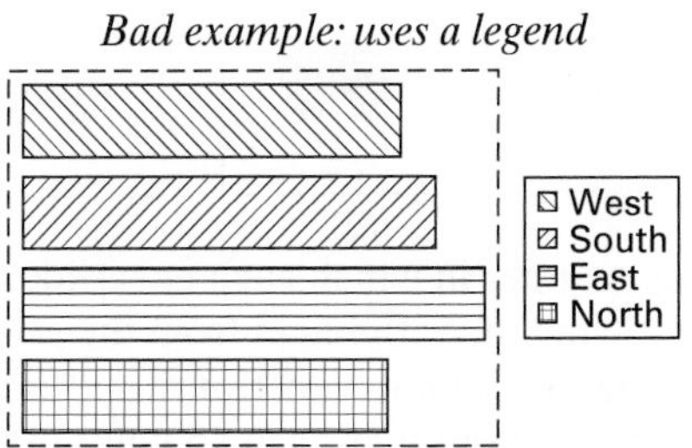

Pointer: The PowerPoint term for the arrow cursor.

Radio button: A small circle that can be selected or deselected to choose options.

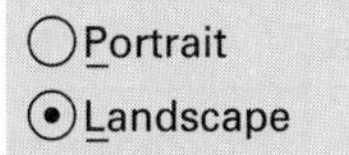

Sentence case: See "Case."

Slide Master: A slide that defines all of the design elements (such as colors, fonts, and other graphics) that will then be used automatically and consistently throughout the entire presentation (the topic of Chapters 3, 4, and 5).

Templates: A series of ready-to-use PowerPoint files with predesigned elements (such as colors, fonts, and other graphics) that will then be used automatically and consistently throughout the entire presentation. We recommend against using PowerPoint templates because they include numerous visual distractions (e.g., all-over graphics, patterns, shimmers, and textures) that make the slides hard to read. Instead, we recommend that you design your own Slide Master (the topic of Chapters 3, 4, and 5).

Text area: The body text placeholder (shown as ❷ on the Placeholder definition on the facing page).

Text box: A moveable, resizable, rectangular container for text that allows you to place text anyplace on the slide—not restricting it to the placeholders defined on the Slide Master.

Thumbnail: A small representation of a graphic image, shown below at actual size.

Transition: The manner in which each new slide appears (e.g., all at once, dissolving in, or flying in from the side). We recommend using the default "No Transition" in which your next slide simply appears all at once, so your audience can focus on your content, not on unnecessary movement on screen (discussed on page 52).

POWERPOINT SHORTCUTS		
	Standard method	**Shortcut method**
		Hold down simultaneously and then release both the Control key (usually labeled Ctrl on your keyboard) and the . . .
Copy	Click Edit → Copy	C key
Cut	Click Edit → Cut	X key
Paste	Click Edit → Paste	V key

GLOSSARY 3

Design and Editing Terms

For the "What To Do" Sections

Accent color: The color you use as a spotlight, drawing your audience's attention to a particular item for emphasis, also known as "spot color" (discussed on pages 35–36).

Agenda: The slide that explains the roadmap, outline, or "table of contents" for your presentation (discussed on page 21).

Audience Memory Curve: A visual representation of what your audience will remember most: that is, the beginning and the end of the presentation (discussed on pages 12–13).

Back-up slides: Slides that explain, or back up, each point on the agenda (discussed on page 22).

Body language: The messages you send nonverbally—including posture, movement, hand and arm gestures, and facial expression (discussed on pages 136–137).

Bullet character: The character of the actual bullet itself, such as a filled circle or a dash (discussed on page 103).

Bullet points: Lines of text that begin with a bullet character (discussed on page 103).

Case: Different choices for capitalization: (1) sentence case (with only the first letter of the first word capitalized, as you would write a sentence), (2) title case (with the first letter of every word capitalized, as you would write a book title), (3) uppercase (with all letters capitalized), and (4) lowercase (nothing capitalized)—discussed on page 43.

Chartjunk: Any gratuitous design element that does not add to your meaning—such as too many colors, 3-D effects, and unnecessary lines and borders (discussed on pages 64–68).

Charts: Slides, such as pie charts, bar charts, or line charts, that make it easier for your audience to comprehend numerical data (the topic of Chapter 6).

Chevron: A diagram used to show a time sequence, as explained on page 80, that looks like this:

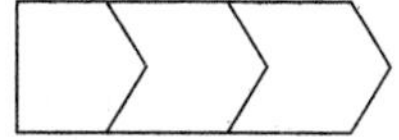

Concept diagrams: Slides that show qualitative concepts visually—such as matrices, flow charts, or pyramids (the topic of Chapter 7).

Deck presentations: Presentations in which you and your audience all have a hard copy of the slides in front of you as you speak (discussed on pages 156–158).

Delivery: Nonverbal behavior including body language, vocal qualities, and interacting with your slides during the presentation (the topics of Chapters 10 and 11).

Diagrams (same as concept diagrams): Slides that show qualitative concepts visually—such as matrices, flow charts, or pyramids (discussed on pages 80–81).

Direct approach: Stating your conclusion at the beginning of your presentation, thus improving your audience's comprehension and saving them time (discussed on page 12).

Font: The kind of typeface, such as Arial or Times New Roman (the topic of Chapter 4).

Font effects: Font options such as shadow or embossed; generally not recommended.

Font styles: Font options such as bold or italics, to be used sparingly for emphasis (discussed on page 43).

Fruit salad effect: The result from using too many colors, making your slide resemble the random colors in a fruit salad (discussed on page 64).

Indirect approach: Saving your conclusion until the end of your presentation, thus making your message harder to follow and taking your audience longer to comprehend it (discussed on pages 12–13).

Legends: An ineffective method of labeling in which the viewers must look back and forth between your chart and a special boxed area called the legend, thereby becoming distracted, confused, and slowed down. Here is an example of a legend, together with an improved example using labels instead (discussed on page 70).

Ineffective legend

West
South
East
North

Effective labels

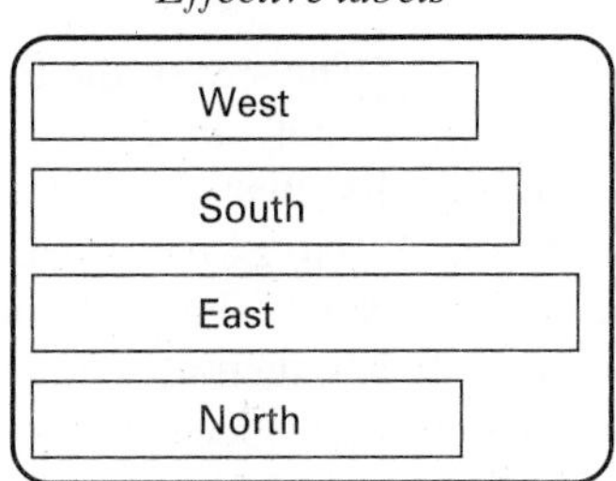

Letterjunk: Any unnecessary fonts, case, and styles that do not add to the slide's meaning (discussed on page 100).

Message titles: The heading or headline at the top of each slide that summarizes the key take-away of that particular slide, usually using an active verb—as opposed to topic titles that simply state the subject of the slide, but don't tell the viewer what message to take away (discussed on pages 23–24).

Bad examples: topic titles	*Good examples: message titles*
Departmental rankings	Department B ranks second
Sales over time	Sales declined in March
Use of materials	Product C uses less iron

Note cards: Cards you refer to during your presentation so you won't have to memorize or read it (discussed on pages 16–17).

Nonverbal delivery: Behavior that includes body language, vocal qualities, and interacting with your slides during the presentation (the topics of Chapters 10 and 11).

Orphan: A word that stands alone because of a random line break (discussed on page 99).

Bad example: orphan	*Improved: no orphan*
low cost of delivery	low cost of delivery

Parallelism: Expressing ideas of equal importance in grammatical structures of equal importance, such as all active verbs or all nouns (discussed on page 102).

Bad example: not parallel	*Good example: parallel*
• Trim the staff • Cut the budget • Better quality control	• Trim the staff • Cut the budget • Improve quality control

Point size: The size of the font, which can range from less than 8 point, virtually unreadable on a slide, to greater than 72 point, too large for most slides. We recommend 28 to 32 point size for titles and 18 to 24 point size for text (discussed on page 44).

Sans serif fonts: Fonts without extenders at the end of each letter stroke, such as Arial. We recommend using sans serif fonts for slides because they have the best readability on an electronic display such as a computer monitor or large screen (discussed on page 42).

Sentence case: The style used to write a sentence, with only the first letter of the first word in upper case (capitalized), and all the other words in lower case (not capitalized) (discussed on page 43).

Serif fonts: Fonts with extenders called "serifs" at the end of each letter stroke, such as Times New Roman or the font you are reading right now. We recommend using serif fonts on paper only, not on slides, because screens have lower display capabilities than paper (discussed on page 42).

Stand-alone sense: Wording that is quickly comprehensible to someone seeing it for the first time (discussed on page 98).

Strategy: Techniques by which you attempt to achieve your desired outcome in the presentation, such as how to persuade your audience or enhance your credibility (the topic of Chapter 1).

Structure: The way you organize your ideas, both verbally and visually, so your audience will best understand you (the topic of Chapter 2).

Support slides: Slides that explain, or back up, each point on the agenda (discussed on page 22).

Telegram language: Wording that omits most articles, auxiliary verbs, and prepositions; recommended for text slides to avoid an overly wordy manuscript style of language (discussed on page 97).

Text slides: Slides (also known as "bullet slides" if they include bullet lists) that are made up of words, as opposed to charts or diagrams (the topic of Chapter 8).

Title case: The capitalization style traditionally used for book titles, with the initial letter of each word capitalized (discussed on page 43).

Trackers: Words or phrases that serve the same purpose as the running header at the top of some book chapters, such as this one, reminding your audience which section of the presentation you are currently covering (discussed on pages 26–27).

Transitions: (1) PowerPoint uses the term "slide transition" to refer to the manner in which each new slide appears—for example, all at once, dissolving in, or flying in from the side (discussed on page 52). We recommend using the default "No Transition" in which your next slide simply appears all at once, so your audience can focus on your content, not on unnecessary movement on screen. (2) Language experts use the term "transition" to mean words or phrases that tie your ideas together—for example, "second," "on the other hand," and "in conclusion" (discussed on page 14).

Bibliography

This bibliography serves both to acknowledge our sources and to provide you with references for additional reading. By design, it is selective, not comprehensive. We have included the best references we could find, even if they're not always the newest. Some of these are "classic"—that is, not recently published but nevertheless crucial—on timeless topics. Others are recent, providing cutting-edge research on more current topics.

Anthony, R., *Talking to The Top: Executive's Guide to Career-Making Presentations.* Englewood Cliffs, NJ: Prentice Hall, 1995.

Bringhurst, R., *The Elements of Typographical Style*. London: Frances Lincoln Ltd, 2004.

Cialdini, R., "Harnessing the Science of Persuasion." *Harvard Business Review.* October, 2001.

French, J. and B. Raven, "The Bases of Social Power," in *Studies in Social Power*, D. Cartwright (ed.). Ann Arbor: University of Michigan Press, 1959.

Howell, J., *Tools for Facilitating*. Seattle: Integrity Press, 1995.

Knapp, M. and J. Hall, *Nonverbal Communication in Human Interaction.* Orlando: Harcourt Brace, 1992.

Larson, R, "Slide Composition for Electronic Presentations," *Journal of Educational Computing Research,* Volume 31, Number 1, 2004.

Mayer, R., *Multimedia Learning.* Cambridge, UK: Cambridge University Press, 2001.

Minto, B., *The Pyramid Principle: Logic in Writing, Thinking, and Problem Solving.* London: Minto International, Inc., 1995.

Munter, M., *Guide to Managerial Communication: Effective Business Writing and Speaking,* 7th ed. Upper Saddle River, NJ: Prentice Hall, 2006.

—— and L. Russell, *Guide to Presentations.* Upper Saddle River, NJ: Prentice Hall, 2007.

—— and M. Netzley, *Guide to Meetings*. Upper Saddle River, NJ: Prentice Hall, 2002.

Robbins, S., *Organizational Behavior: Concepts and Controversies.* 11th ed. Englewood Cliffs, NJ: Prentice Hall, 2005.

Thomas, J., *Guide to Managerial Persuasion and Influence.* Upper Saddle River, NJ: Prentice Hall, 2004.

Toogood, G. *The Articulate Executive: Learn to Look, Act, and Sound Like a Leader.* New York: McGraw-Hill, 1996.

Tufte, E., *The Cognitive Style of PowerPoint.* Cheshire, CT: Graphics Press, 2003.

——, *The Visual Display of Quantitative Information.* Cheshire, CT: Graphics Press, 2001.

Vetter, R *et al.*, "Using Color and Text in Multimedia Projections," *IEEE Multimedia,* Winter 1995.

White, J., *Color for Impact: How Color Can Get Your Message Across—or Get in the Way.* Berkeley, CA: Strathmoor Press, 1997.

Williams, R., *The Non-Designer's Design Book: Design & Typographic Principles for the Visual Novice,* 2nd ed. Berkeley, CA: Peachpit Press, 2003.

Zelazny, G., *Say It With Charts: The Executive's Guide to Visual Communication.* 4th ed. New York: McGraw-Hill, 2001.

——, *Say It With Presentations: How to Design and Deliver Successful Business Presentations*. New York: McGraw-Hill, 2000.

Index

C

D

E

F

O

P

Q

R

S

T